THE RESTART EFFECT

The Restart Effect

Evaluation of a labour market programme for unemployed people

Michael White and Jane Lakey

Policy Studies Institute
London

PSI PUBLISHING

The publishing imprint of the independent
POLICY STUDIES INSTITUTE
100 Park Village East, London NW1 3SR
Telephone: 071-387 2171; Fax: 071-388 0914

© **Policy Studies Institute 1992**

ISBN 0 85374 554 4

PSI Research Report 739

A CIP catalogue record of this book is available from the British Library.

1 2 3 4 5 6 7 8 9

PSI publications are available from
BEBC Distribution Ltd
P O Box 1496, Poole, Dorset, BH12 3YD

Books will normally be despatched within 24 hours. Cheques should be made payable to BEBC Distribution Ltd.

Credit card and telephone/fax orders may be placed on the following freephone numbers:

FREEPHONE: 0800 262260
FREEFAX: 0800 262266

Booktrade representation (UK & Eire):
Book Representation and Distribution Ltd (BRAD)
244a London Road, Hadleigh, Essex SS7 2DE

PSI subscriptions are available from PSI's subscription agent
Carfax Publishing Company Ltd
P O Box 25, Abingdon, Oxford OX14 3UE

Laserset by Policy Studies Institute
Printed in Great Britain by BPCC Wheatons Ltd, Exeter

Contents

Acknowledgements

The analysis on which this report is based was commissioned by the Employment Service.

The authors are grateful for the help and encouragement provided by Len Dawes and Margaret Hersee, the liaison officers for the study, and by the Steering Group chaired by Linda Ammon. We are also grateful for comments on the drafting of the report from various members of the Employment Service and the Employment Department, and from Jon Hales of Social and Community Planning Research (SCPR).

Within the Policy Studies Institute, the report owes much to the advice and help of Joan Payne.

The content and conclusions of the report remain the sole responsibility of the authors.

Executive Summary

1 The Study

1.1 The Restart Cohort Study was designed to answer two questions:

a. What were the effects of Restart?

b. How were its effects achieved?

1.2 The study was carried out by means of a national sample of unemployed people approaching a six months duration of claim. Data from two survey interviews (at about 12 and 18 months after start of claim) were linked to information from administrative records, and from national computer databases. Complex precautions were taken to protect individuals' identities.

1.3 A control group (to whose members the Restart process was not applied) was used to evaluate the effects of Restart.

1.4 The design and methods of the study provided a direct assessment of the effects of Restart upon individuals. To assess wider labour market effects requires additional economic assumptions and/or comparison with findings of macroeconomic studies of the labour market.

1.5 The study took place in 1989-90, and the assessment does not directly take into account changes in Restart, and in labour market conditions, which have occurred since that time.

2 Restart effects

2.1 The main findings of the research are summarised in Table 1.

2.2 The research indicates that the Restart process had significant effects on the reduction of claiming and time taken to leave the unemployment register. The best estimate of reduction in time claiming for respondents who went through the Restart process was around five per cent.

2.3 This, however, does not take full account of the proportion remaining on the claimant register until the end of the study period. Restart appeared significantly to reduce this proportion, by comparison with the control group.

2.4 Restart had its most substantial effect in reducing the time taken to leave the register. This effect did not translate fully into reduction of total time claiming (2.2 above), because many jobs obtained were relatively short-lived and were followed by flows back to unemployment.

2.5 Restart significantly reduced the average time taken to enter jobs or self-employment. The effect on the average time spent in employment over the period was less clear, but there was some indication that the advantage of Restart participants in this respect developed progressively over the period of one year.

2.6 There was no evidence that Restart affected the occupational level, wages, or stability of employment in the jobs obtained.

2.7 Restart significantly increased the average amount of time spent on Employment Training (ET) and other government programmes, and reduced the average time taken to enter such programmes, over the whole year of the study.

2.8 The effects of Restart on movements into a non-claimant but non-employed status appeared to differ in the short-term (six-12 months after claim) and in the medium-term (12-18 months after claim). In the earlier period, Restart appeared to reduce the entry time to a non-claimant, non-employed status and to increase the time spent in that status. In the later period, this tendency appeared to be reversed.

2.9 For men in the sample, Restart did not appear to influence leaving the register at a very early stage (before or immediately upon the counselling interview). For women, however, there was an indication of a specific Restart effect on early exits.

2.10 The overall effect of Restart (in terms of leaving the register) appeared by about one month after the Restart interview. As already indicated (see 2.3 above), it was still clearly present at about 12 months after this interview.

2.11 There was no evidence (with the possible exception of 2.9 above) of different Restart effects for men and for women. Nor were different Restart effects found for different age groups. The scope for examining such differences was, however, rather limited (by the size of the control group) and their possibility cannot be excluded.

2.12 The Restart effect was generally of about the same order of magnitude as effects such as qualifications, marital status, presence of young children, local labour market conditions, etc. The only factors which were clearly more important in influencing outcomes were the gender and age of the individual.

2.13 It was possible to check the subsequent claiming of those who were unwilling to be interviewed in the survey or could not be contacted. On average these spent less time as claimants than did people who were interviewed. This was found not to affect significantly the conclusions concerning Restart.

2.14 The main reasons for moving into a non-claimant, non-employed status were concerned with benefit entitlement, childcare, and ill-health, but there were also numerous short-term spells of inactivity following termination of employment or ET.

2.15 An assessment was made of the financial position of those moving into non-claimant, non-employed status for reasons connected with benefit entitlement. The average financial position of this group appeared to be more satisfactory than that of people remaining as claimants.

3 How Restart works

3.1 Restart does not depend upon any one type of effect. It achieves its overall results by increasing movement into both jobs and ET or other training programmes and, in the short-term only, into non-claimant, non-meployed status.

3.2 There appeared to be little if any impact of the Restart process prior to the Restart interview. On the other hand, a small proportion of the sample reported that they did take some action on job search as a result of the letter asking them to attend a Restart interview.

3.3 The Restart interviews (plus, in one in five cases, a second interview) acted as a gateway to a wide range of programmes, services and follow-up actions. In the great majority of interviews, several possibilities from this range were discussed, and direct assistance from the Restart counsellor (for example, to contact an employer or to arrange an ET assessment) was common.

3.4 There were numerous indications that, in the Restart process, particular attention was paid to those who were likely to be at a competitive disadvantage in the labour market, such as those with disabilities or health problems, older workers, or those with particularly low prior levels of employment. People with various disadvantages also, on average, tended to be more appreciative of Restart, although there was not a simple correspondence between those getting various forms of help and perceptions of that help.

The groups which appeared, in general, to receive less suggestions through Restart were women and older workers. (But see 2.11 above, which indicated no overall differences in outcomes linked to Restart for women or for older workers.)

3.5 There was no indication that Restart in general achieved its effect by stimulating a higher level of job search activity or by increasing wage flexibility or other forms of flexibility in the job market. There was some indication however that those who were submitted to a placement, but not actually placed, may subsequently have had above-average levels of job search.

3.6 Restart can be interpreted as a process which 'adds value' to programmes and services for unemployed people and achieves its effects by a combination of numerous actions.

Table 1   Summary of main findings

Measure of effect	Sample used	Effect of Restart
Change in time claiming	Whole	Reduction
Time to leave claimant register	Whole	Reduction
Change in time claiming	Stage 1 respondents	Reduction
Time to leave claimant register	Stage 1 respondents	Reduction
Time in employment	Stage 1 respondents	None
Whether entered ET	Stage 1 respondents	None
Time to enter ET	Stage 1 respondents	Reduction
Time in non-activity	Stage 1 respondents	Increase
Time in employment	Stage 2 respondents	Inconclusive
Time to enter employment	Stage 2 respondents	Reduction
Time in ET	Stage 2 respondents	Increase
Time to enter ET	Stage 2 respondents	Reduction
Time in non-activity	Stage 2 respondents	None
Time to enter non-activity	Stage 2 respondents	None

1 The Research Study

During 1986 a new system was introduced to review periodically the position of people who continued to be registered as unemployed. Known as Restart, the system's central feature was an interview between the unemployed person and a Restart counsellor. The interview was also intended to link unemployed people into a range of other services within the wider system of provision for unemployment. Initially introduced as a pilot scheme, Restart during 1987-88 developed into a national system of six-monthly interviews for all unemployed claimants.

The responsibility for operating the Restart system has rested with the Employment Service, initially a division of the Employment Department Group, and subsequently a government agency. In 1989 the Employment Service commissioned Social and Community Planning Research to carry out a cohort survey of a national sample of unemployed people who were reaching the time of an initial Restart interview. A first survey interview with the sample took place in Summer 1989. A follow-up survey interview took place about six months later, in Spring 1990.

The Policy Studies Institute was commissioned to play an advisory role in the design of the interview questionnaires, to carry out the main analysis of the survey data, and to produce the chief report of the findings. Most of PSI's analysis was carried out during the period December 1990-May 1991.

The timing of the study may be an important consideration in the interpretation of findings. Restart has evolved further since the time of the study; what we describe is what existed at that time. For example, in this study we usually refer to the staff conducting Restart interviews as 'Restart counsellors', the term in use at the time of the study. Subsequently, Restart interviewing has been merged into the role of Claimant Advisers at Benefit Offices (which are integrated with the old Jobcentres), so the term used in this report is no longer current. Appendix 1 provides a short description of Restart, provided by the Employment Service, including description of changes taking place in 1990-91.

There has also been a period of economic recession between the time of the survey and 1992. The possible significance of these economic changes is discussed in Chapter 8.

Aims of the inquiry

The formal aims of the study to be carried out by PSI were defined in the Employment Service's research brief as to:

'a) describe and measure the impact of Restart on its clients, the operation of the labour market and its institutions; and

b) describe how Restart is achieving changes.'

In short, this was an evaluation study, intended to answer the question: What difference did Restart make? The analysis, and this report, have accordingly been focused upon providing answers to this question.

It may be helpful to preview very briefly the nature of those answers. Restart is a broad process applied across the whole span of continuing unemployed claimants, and it is linked to a range of measures provided by the labour market and benefit services. Its impact cannot therefore be captured in any single measure. Our assessment considers impacts upon the claiming of benefits, obtaining jobs or placements in Employment Training or other training programmes, moving into a non-claimant, non-employed status, job search (both quantitative and qualitative), characteristics of new jobs, and flexibility. Further, it considers the outcomes at two separate times, and for some aspects compares each with a longer previous period or 'baseline'.

Although chiefly focusing on the effect of Restart upon outcomes, the Restart Cohort Study was also intended to *clarify the way Restart worked.* Here the questions are more diffuse. From the side of the providers of Restart, one would presumably want to know which (if any) parts of the process had the greatest leverage on outcomes. Indeed, could it be that some aspects of Restart had contrary outcomes to other parts? From the viewpoint of the recipients, the questions perhaps concern the *salience* or perceived helpfulness of various parts of Restart, and the links between such subjective impressions and the objective outcomes.

It should perhaps be mentioned here that the role of initiatives offering review, counselling, information services, and so on, has in the past few years become a focus of considerable interest among labour market specialists concerned with unemployment. This will be discussed further in Chapter 2. The point is that, as well as providing an assessment of a particular programme, this study may be valuable for the light it sheds on issues, concerning the design of labour market services, which are of wider interest.

A final, subsidiary aim of the study has been to develop a database on unemployment which offers scope for further analysis. The Restart Cohort Survey was in fact much the most extensive survey of unemployment carried out since 1980.[1] Many aspects on which data were collected in the survey have been considered only briefly and superficially in this report, or have not been considered at all: they were not directly relevant to an evaluation of the Restart process. However, efforts have been made to provide an easy-to-use version of the dataset which will encourage further analysis for other purposes. Furthermore, the dataset is far more extensive than customary surveys. It incorporates administrative data from the Restart interviews, claimant history data from the Employment Department's JUVOS computer system, and local labour market data from the NOMIS system. There is scope for further information to be added, and, indeed, some follow-up studies have already been undertaken or are planned. The Restart Cohort Study database should be an asset for many types of study of unemployment for some years to come.

Structure and presentation of the report
The report has two preliminary chapters, followed by five chapters presenting the findings of the analysis, and a final chapter of discussion and conclusion. The present chapter provides background information about the survey itself and the analysis methods used, while Chapter 2 discusses the evolution of labour market conditions and institutions and provides some descriptive background about the members of the sample. Chapter 1 (especially its first half) is essential to an appreciation of the results presented later, but Chapter 2 may be regarded as optional. The idea of the first two chapters is largely to simplify the presentation of the results, in later chapters.

Chapters 3 to 7 present the results of the analyses and their piecemeal interpretation. As far as possible, these analyses have been presented in non-technical language. It has to be appreciated however that the task of the analysis has been a complex one, and it was necessary to use fairly sophisticated, although standard, tools of multivariate statistical analysis. The methods, and the reasons for selecting them, are described later in the present chapter, but the reader preferring to skip that material should find sufficient description of what was done in the later chapters along with the results.

It has been decided not to include the detailed statistical results of the various multivariate analyses within the report. Those wishing to have copies of the original computer outputs for all or part of the analyses are requested to contact the authors. Crucial details of the statistical findings are provided in notes to the chapters, which also contain literature references. In addition, we have sought to provide convenient visual summaries of the most important results from the multivariate analyses in chart form.

The concluding discussion and overall interpretation of the findings is presented in Chapter 8. This differs from the Executive Summary placed at the start of this report, in that it goes somewhat beyond the findings and offers a wider consideration of the possible implications.

An outline of the surveys and dataset
The next section of this chapter provides a non-technical outline of the surveys carried out and of the dataset which has been created.

An inflow sample
Surveys of unemployment are based on samples of two broad types: stock samples and flow samples. A stock sample covers a cross-section of people who are unemployed at a given time, but may be confined to (say) those with more than six months of unemployment. Such a sample will include considerable numbers of people with very long incomplete spells of unemployment, and will generally incorporate a wide variation in the duration of unemployment. A flow sample, by contrast, restricts the sample to a narrow band by selecting from people who are just entering unemployment, or who are just completing a certain period of unemployment.

A stock sample results in greater variation over many of the factors influencing unemployment, and this gives it some advantage if the aim is to explain what happens in unemployment in a broad way. Conversely, a flow sample restricts variation and this is beneficial if one wishes to focus upon the operation of one or two factors, with minimum interference from other factors. A flow sample is therefore preferable for an evaluation study such as the present one.

The Restart Cohort Study was based upon a sample of unemployed claimants (that is, of people registering for benefit on grounds of unemployment), all of whom were approaching six months of unemployment. They were selected as an integral part of the Restart process. At the time, each unemployed claimant received an initial Restart interview at approximately six months of unemployment (and each six months thereafter), and a letter asking the individual to attend interview was sent out about two weeks in advance. The survey sample was identified in the Employment Service's local offices as the list of those eligible for the six-month Restart interview was prepared.

If for some reason a person did not attend the Restart interview, they still remained in the sample, once selected. So it is a sample of the inflow to Restart, not of the outflow from Restart. This means that the effect of the whole Restart process, including the effect of the initial letter before the interview, can be assessed.

It is important to note that this sample concerns only the inflow at six months of unemployment. Not only does it exclude the short-term unemployed, who never entered the Restart process, but it also excludes the effect of Restart upon those having Restart interviews after longer periods of continuous unemployment, from one year upwards.

A national unclustered sample
Every Employment Service local office throughout Britain was involved in drawing the sample. Moreover, they drew individuals from the whole six-month Restart inflow without restrictions. The sample was, therefore, unusual in being both national and spatially unclustered.[2]

A random sample linked to the JUVOS Cohort database
The method of identifying members of the sample from within the inflow lists was by means of the terminating digit sequences of

National Insurance (NI) numbers. The specified digit sequences corresponded to those used by the JUVOS Cohort database. This is a national computerised system which maintains a cumulative record of the starting and ending dates of unemployment claims for five per cent of the population. The NI digit sequences used by JUVOS to select individuals are known to result in a random five per cent sample (since all individuals have an equal chance of being allocated these digit sequences). By using the same NI digit sequences, the Restart sample (a) was assured of being random, and (b) could be linked to the information on the JUVOS database. It became possible to attach to each individual in the sample a complete claiming history commencing with any claim current in 1982, when the JUVOS Cohort began.

A random control group within the sample

The sample for the study contained a 'control group', members of which were *not* sent a letter inviting them to a Restart interview. To ensure as far as possible that the selection of control group members would be random, they were identified by means of previously specified NI digit sequences, just as the main sample members were. Moreover, these NI digit sequences formed part of the overall set of NI digit sequences by which the JUVOS Cohort as a whole is defined, so that the selection process for the Restart group and the control group was of precisely the same form.

If any members of the control group asked for a Restart interview, however, they were accorded one (the implications of this requirement will be discussed further below). Also, membership of the control group did not limit access to programmes and services for unemployed poeple, by routes other than Restart. For example, they could still make use of all Jobcentre services or apply directly for Employment Training. Further, their exclusion from Restart only applied to the initial Restart interview at the stage of six months from claim; if they were still unemployed at 12 months from claim, they would be included in the full Restart process.

Three points about the control group design are crucial for the study and need to be specially emphasised:

a) Because the Restart process is applied to all those reaching six months of unemployment, an evaluation would have been *impossible* if a control group sample had not been used.

b) Because the control group members had access to all other programmes and services by all other routes, the study was correctly designed to measure the *net or additional effect* of Restart.

c) Because the control group members would miss only the initial (six-month) Restart interview, the Restart effect measured is limited to that initial interview and the related processes.

Sample stratification by Restart 'action

The sample design incorporated a number of groups or strata, with varying proportions of individuals across strata. The reason for this was to have adequate numbers for separate analysis within strata of particular interest, while reducing the survey costs where excess numbers were available for a stratum.

The stratification was by what we here call Restart actions. (Within the Employment Service these were referred to as 'menu items' but this may be confusing to others outside the Service.) The term we propose to use derives from the procedures used by the Restart counsellors. Each individual to whom a Restart letter is sent has to be allocated subsequently to an 'action', which represents the initial outcome of the Restart interview. Three examples out of the eight possible actions indicate what is meant (for further details, see Appendix 2):

a. *Placed* (the individual obtained a positive outcome such as a job, a place on Employment Training, or a place in a Jobclub, as a direct result of the Restart process).

b. *Submitted* (submitted to a placement, as above, but there was no positive result at the time of completing the record).

c. *Excused interview* (the individual was given permission not to attend the interview; this could arise, for example, because he or she had just obtained a job).

This stratification was probably the least effective aspect of the survey design. The proportions recorded under the various options turned out, over the period of the sampling, to be rather different from what had been expected on the basis of past statistics, so that there was less scope for useful stratification than was hoped. In addition, a fall in unemployment at the time of sampling reduced the flows into Restart. In the end, four of the options, plus the control group, were sampled at 100 per cent. The remaining four were sampled at a fraction of three in four (75 per cent).

It should be noted that, so far as local Employment Service staff were concerned, sampling was at 100 per cent throughout; selection on the basis of strata was applied by Employment Service staff centrally.

Survey interviews

A potential source of confusion, in attempting to describe the study, is that individuals in our sample receive both 'Restart interviews' (also sometimes referred to as counselling interviews) and 'Restart survey interviews'. In order to avoid confusion as far as possible, we shall always from now on speak of 'Restart interviews' and 'survey interviews'.

Two stages of survey interviewing

Those retained in the sample after stratification were sent a letter by the Employment Service explaining the purpose of the survey and the way it was to be conducted, and were offered the chance of opting out of the survey. The names and addresses of those not opting out were then passed to Social and Community Planning Research (SCPR) for interviewing.

At the first survey interview, individuals were asked whether they would be willing to take part in a further survey interview after another six months. Those that agreed to do so were re-contacted if possible and a second survey interview took place. Both survey interviews were conducted by means of a highly structured questionnaire; a short self-completion questionnaire, concerned with personal attitudes, was also used on each occasion. The average survey interview time was about 45 minutes.

The timetable for the survey

As explained, the sample was drawn a short time before the first Restart interview became due. About three-four months were needed to carry out the various stages of sample selection and processing, to the point where the letter explaining the survey could be sent out. This therefore would have been received by sampled individuals well after the initial Restart interview, but well before the letter inviting the individual (if still unemployed) to a second Restart interview. It was particularly important to carry out the first survey interview in advance of the second Restart interview, otherwise recollections of the initial Restart interview would have been confused with those of the second one.

In general, the first survey interview took place about five but less than six months after the initial Restart interview, or about 11 but less than 12 months after the start of the unemployment claim in question. The second survey interview followed on with an interval of about six months, and so took place at about five months after the second Restart interview (if any), 11 months after the first Restart interview, and 17 months after commencement of the unemployment claim.

To obtain a sufficiently large sample, it was necessary to accumulate the inflow to the Restart process over a period. Restart inflow lists are made up fortnightly. In fact, sampling continued for eight Restart lists or a period of 16 weeks, in September to December 1988. The survey interviewing was likewise spread out in batches corresponding to the original lists. The fist survey interviews took place in September 1989.

Data linking and protection of confidentiality

An aim of the survey was to create a linked database with survey interview information combined with administrative information recorded at or following the Restart interview (notably, the Restart action codes, described above), and information on claiming histories from the JUVOS Cohort. Such linking has to be carried out by the use of individual identification numbers. However, an important consideration was the protection of the individual against any possible misuse of the linked information.

NI numbers, identifying individuals on the administrative records and the JUVOS Cohort data, were passed to the Employment Service, who replaced them with a new personal identification number. The latter, but not the NI numbers, were passed with the administrative and JUVOS data to SCPR. SCPR possessed both the Employment Service's identification number and the serial number used on the survey questionnaires, but never had access to NI numbers. In passing the administrative, JUVOS and survey data to PSI for analysis, SCPR attached the survey serial number and removed the Employment Service number. PSI used the survey serial number only, and never had access either to NI numbers or to the Employment Service's identification numbers.

The administrative information contained a travel-to-work-area code for each individual. This was used by PSI to attach summary local labour market data from the NOMIS computer system at Durham University.

Sample size and response rate

The full dataset passed to PSI consisted of 8,925 cases. These included 5,200 individuals who had completed the first survey interview, while 3,725 had not been interviewed for a variety of reasons such as refusal, movement to a different address or difficulty of contact. Finally, some 3,690 completed a second survey interview as well.

The overall net response rate at the first survey interview was assessed by SCPR (after allowing for opt-out, untraceable addresses, etc.) at 71 per cent. Of these, some 75 per cent were also interviewed again in the follow-up by SCPR.

Not all of those who took part in a survey interview could be used in the final analysis by PSI. In particular, it was most important to eliminate any cases from the sample where the dates of the claim before Restart sampling did not conform to the criteria for inclusion in the sample. People with appreciably longer or shorter spells of unemployment than the six months used to define this study would have, on average, substantially worse, or better, chances of leaving unemployment than the average for the Restart sample. With the existence of the JUVOS Cohort data, this aspect could be checked directly, and in fact some 448 cases were removed because they did not conform to the sampling criteria: they had either much more than six months of unemployment at the time of sampling, or (less commonly) much less than six months.[3] A number of other cases were also removed, either because they lacked JUVOS Cohort data, or because they could not be matched to travel-to-work areas.

The numbers of cases actually used for analysis, after eliminating the cases described above, were as follows:

Total issued sample: 8,189 cases

Interviewed at first stage: 4,807 cases

Interviewed at both first and second stages: 3,419 cases.

These numbers were a little smaller than originally planned. The shortfall occurred largely because during the period when the sample was being created (March-June 1989), the demand for labour was particularly strong and the flow into Restart was considerably diminished. Nevertheless, this remains one of the largest surveys of unemployment undertaken in Britain.

Effective size of control group
The reduced flow into unemployment also affected the size of the control group. It had originally been expected that some 600 control group members might be interviewed. However, among the 8,189 cases forming the basis for the analysis, there were only 528 control group members. Of these, 323 were interviewed at the first stage of the survey and 246 at the second stage.

Further, as earlier explained, members of the control group were able to have Restart interviews if they asked for them. Administrative mistakes might also have led to some people who should have been in the control group being called into the Restart procedure at some stage. It was found that of the 323 control group members having a first-stage survey interview, 83 either stated that they had had a Restart interview or were noted as having had a Restart interview on the administrative records.[4] That left 240 people from the original control group who received a survey interview and (as originally intended) did not receive a Restart interview. Similarly, 60 of the control group interviewed at the second stage of the survey appeared to have taken part in the initial Restart interview, leaving 186 who had not.

Summary of study design
It may be helpful to recapitulate the main features of the study design. These were:
- The large size of the overall sample
- Focusing upon those nearing six months of unemployment
- Following them up over one year through two survey interviews
- Linking the sample to administrative and computer records (even for those not interviewed in the survey), to provide information particularly about claiming and about Restart 'actions'
- Inclusion of a randomly selected control group, members of which were not asked to take part in the Restart interviews.

Of these features, the last was the most crucial for meeting the aims of the study.

Analysis of the data and presentation of findings
In this final section of Chapter 1, we outline our approach to the task of data analysis and explain some of the main problems which had to be resolved. Those primarily interested in the findings could by-pass this section, as later chapters have (it is hoped) been written in a way which requires no technical background nor any reference to this section. Those reading this section will encounter some repetition, in later chapters, of points made here, although they will be made here in greater depth. This repetition is unavoidable in order to meet the needs of readers with different priorities.

Control group method
The chief method used to obtain an assessment of the effects of Restart was the control group design, leading to comparisons of outcomes between the control group and those passing through the normal Restart process. Control group design is widely regarded as the most reliable method of assessing the effects of labour market programmes.[5]

This type of comparison is often referred to in the econometric literature on programme evaluation as the 'experimental' method. The analogy is with a medical or psychological experiment in which individuals are allocated randomly either to a 'treatment' group or to a 'control (no treatment)' group. It has to be appreciated, however, that in a large-scale study taking place in a 'real world' context, it is not possible to achieve the degree of control over conditions which exists in a clinical or laboratory experiment. Hence, even with a control group design, there is the possibility of sources of bias being introduced and affecting the comparisons. It remains important, therefore, to test for the presence of such bias.

Control group definition and testing
The chief potential problem with the control group lies in the effect of its members entering Restart procedures. As described earlier, rather more than one in four of those intended for the control group appear to have had Restart interviews. In part, this could have arisen through mistakes in the Restart office, with (say) a person's name not being

withdrawn from the list of those who should be sent a letter about Restart. In part, it could have arisen from people asking for a Restart interview when aware that they appeared to have been overlooked. What is the effect of including these cases within the control group, or alternatively what is the effect of withdrawing them from the control group?

There are no *a priori* answers to these questions. It is conceivable that (a) retaining the Restart participants within the control group leads to an underestimate of Restart effects, (b) retaining them leads to an overestimate of Restart effects, (c) withdrawing them leads to an underestimate of Restart effects, (d) withdrawing them leads to an overestimate of Restart effects.[6] It is also possible that entry into Restart procedures from the control group is a random process; in that case, it makes no difference to the comparisons whether the Restart entrants are retained in the control group or removed from the control group.

What is needed, therefore, is a practical assessment of the degree of bias, if any, arising from the movement of control group members into Restart. To provide this assessment, we carried out a series of related investigations.

a) If those entering Restart from the control group are a non-random selection, then it would be likely that the remaining control group (after removing the Restart entrants) would differ from the Restart group in some of the characteristics connected with outcomes after unemployment, such as age, gender, qualifications, and so on. Similarly, if the original control group (before movement into Restart) contained some bias, then differences in such characteristics might again be expected to emerge. By comparing the relationships of a set of such characteristics with Restart group/control group, we can therefore obtain a test for the presence of bias.

An analysis of this form was therefore carried out, both for the original or 'inclusive' control group, and for the 'reduced' or 'exclusive' control group from which Restart entrants were withdrawn. Membership of the control group was taken as a binary dependent variable, and the other variables, representing personal characteristics, human capital, local labour market conditions, etc., were used to 'predict' control group membership through a logistic regression equation. The results of these analyses are presented in detail in Appendix 3. The findings, in short, were that on neither definition of the control group was there any statistical evidence of differences in characteristics between the control group and the Restart group. Further, the analyses yielded closely similar results whichever definition of the control group was used. There was, therefore, no indication of a bias being introduced into the control group.

b) Although the control group might be random or unbiased in terms of its background characteristics, it might still be biased in terms of its current behaviour. In particular, the econometric literature pays considerable attention to the possible biassing influences of unobserved 'motivational' differences between programme participants and non-participants. It seems reasonable to assume that motivation would, in unemployment, express itself through job search. 'Self-selection' into Restart might be linked to above-average, or to below-average, levels of job search. In testing this we would, of course, have to control for other characteristics which could influence levels of job search.

The relationship between Restart and job search activity was, in any case, one of the matters which had to be investigated in the research, and the findings are reported in Chapter 7. For present purposes, the chief point is simply that no statistically significant relationship between Restart participation and amount of job search was found. This also means that no relationship was found between control group membership and job search. Once again, therefore, there was no evidence of a bias being introduced into the control group.

c) We also examined differences in attitudes towards unemployment between the control group (in each of its two definitions) and the Restart group, since these might conceivably tap into aspects of motivation not reflected in measures of job search. One potential bias being tested was that those entering Restart from the control group might have had distinctive attitudes (which could perhaps have affected outcomes at a later stage). Equally, and more importantly in the case of the 'inclusive' or original control group, if late or 'non-standard' entry to Restart had adverse effects, these might have been expected to have led to some negative attitudes.

A set of 13 attitudinal measures, relating to various aspects of unemployment, was available from the survey. Each of these was cross-tabulated with control group membership and a test of association was performed; this was repeated with each of the two definitions of the control group.[7] Two of the 26 tables (one in each set of 13) produced statistically significant results, but the differences identified were both small and lacking in any practical interpretation. The conclusion to be drawn, again, was that there was no evidence of a bias being introduced into the control group.[8]

Taken together, these analyses suggest that (a) the control group as originally formed was unbiassed, and (b) entry into Restart from the control group was unlikely to have introduced any subsequent bias into the assessment of outcomes.

This in practice leaves us free to use whichever of the two control group definitions is more convenient. For the majority of the analyses, we have preferred to use the 'exclusive' or reduced control group. The main reason for doing so is its presentational convenience. It is much easier to think in terms of a direct correspondence between control group and non-participation in Restart, than to think in terms of a control group which has been partially 'diluted' by Restart participation.

The exception to this is in the case of analyses using all the original sample, including the non-respondents. Where there was no survey interview, there was of course no self-report of Restart participation. In these analyses, therefore, we used the 'inclusive' or original definition of the control group, because we simply could not have applied the 'exclusive' definition in the case of the non-respondents.

If there were a bias resulting from movement into Restart from the control group, then this should lead to systematic differences when otherwise identical analyses are repeated with the two different control group definitions. As our final precaution, we have repeated all the main analyses of outcomes after Restart (except those including the non-respondents), using the 'inclusive' control group definition. A table summarizing the comparative results is shown in Appendix 3. The two sets of analyses, taken as a whole, led to broadly similar conclusions; there were particular differences of magnitude, but not of direction, and the differences were not systematic (they did not all point one way). For the sake of simplicity, the text of the report generally presents the analyses with the 'exclusive' control group as the basis of comparison, but details of the results using the alternative control group definition are provided in notes to the report as well as in Appendix 3.

Possible administrative bias

In a laboratory or clinical experiment, care is taken to prevent knowledge of the treatment being applied biassing the outcomes. In an administrative setting such as in the present study, this degree of experimental purity is not attainable. It is conceivable, therefore, that staff in the local offices, having noted that particular individuals were members either of the Restart group or of the control group, could have treated them differently from normal.

No direct statistical assessment of such a possibility can be made. It was partly for this reason that staff from the PSI research team visited local offices to observe Restart in operation. Our view based on this observation was that biassed treatment of those in the survey was unlikely. Those in the survey sample formed a small part of a much larger case-load at any local office (about 1 in 100 of those interviewed over a period). The pressures of the case-load (resulting in a fairly continuous stream of interviews) in our view left little scope for the Restart counsellors to give special treatment to those in the survey sample.

Further, the Restart counsellors had no knowledge of the aims of the study or of the outcome measures which were to be examined. The procedures to which they work emphasise intermediate outcomes (especially moving to a clear action outcome in each case) rather than the longer-term measures which we used.

Outcome measures

A critical step in any evaluation is to define the outcome measures which are to be considered. Much of the econometric literature on programme evaluation (which is largely American) focuses upon wage outcomes. The customary procedure is to compare wages after participation in the programme with wages before, for both programme participants and non-participants. This focus upon wage outcomes results from underlying economic theory which associates wage gains with human capital and marginal productivity increases; these theoretical connections also provide a framework for making inferences from individual effects to wider labour market effects (for a recent discussion, see Disney and colleagues[9]).

A focus upon wage outcomes, however, would not be either appropriate or feasible in the case of the evaluation of Restart. In policy terms, adding to human capital does not appear to be a direct aim or criterion of the Restart programme. In terms of economic concepts, the function of the Restart programme would be, rather, to increase the effective labour supply. This could (under some conditions) operate through a reduction in reservation wages of job-seekers[10] and it could also have the effect of reducing the general wage level in the labour market. It is not clear, therefore, what the wage objectives of Restart should be, if any. It would of course be of considerable general interest to estimate the effect of Restart participation upon wages. But the relatively small size of the control group, coupled with the limitations of available wage data, in any case made such an analysis impractical to pursue.[11]

The policy aims of Restart can reasonably be interpreted in terms of helping and motivating individuals to move out of their unemployed status, including moves into government programmes like ET or moves into non-employed, non-claimant status as well as into jobs. Rather than focus upon wages, therefore, we have in our analyses focused upon outcomes defined in terms of employment status.

It seemed reasonable to measure outcomes primarily through time in claimant unemployment, and in other labour market statuses, as the key outcome measures. Time is one of the standard means of expressing the severity of unemployment (as in 'long-term unemployment') and is closely involved in measuring the costs of unemployment. Measures of time are statistically tractable and, in fact, are closely related to probabilistic notions.

Much research into unemployment in recent years has used the method of survival analysis, which is concerned with the elapsed time before a transitional event occurs, such as a move from unemployment into some other status. Depending on the point of view, one can consider such an analysis as being concerned with either 'exit-times' (from the initial status) or with 'entry-times' (into the new status). This also fits well with the notion of 'flows' into, and out of, unemployment. An analysis of exit-times from unemployment seems particularly appropriate in relation to Restart, because it would reflect gains in efficiency or 'throughput' in the system. Furthermore, the statistical method of survival analysis takes fully into account those individuals who remain in unemployment at the end of the period of observation, as well as the variations in exit-times. It does so by constructing a distribution of exit-times while, so to speak, fitting the incomplete observations into this distribution. It therefore makes use of time data with maximum efficiency.[12]

A period of time can, in principle, be comprehensively assessed by applying survival analysis to all the transitions which take place within it. One would look not only at the initial move out of unemployment, for example, but also at moves back into unemployment at subsequent points, and at second or later moves out of unemployment again. (Such an approach is exemplified in a recent study of youth labour market transitions in Ireland by Breen.[13]) Despite the attractions of a unified analysis method, however, we decided not to adopt this approach. The chief reason was that, in order to do so, one would have to move from an analysis in terms of individuals to an analysis in terms of transitions (an individual can be represented by more than one transition within an analysis). There are advantages in terms of simplicity of presentation if the unit of analysis remains the individual. Similarly, the variety of transitions to be included would have risen sharply and increased the complexity of the account. Finally, these more elaborate forms of survival analysis raise technical issues, especially the problem of the correlation of within-person statuses, which would have added to the difficulty of the exposition.

We therefore confine our use of survival analysis solely to the initial transition out of unemployment, and to the initial transitions into a job, into a government programme such as ET, and into a non-claimant (but non-employed) status. This focus upon initial transitions means that the unit of analysis always remains the individual.

This decision means that the survival analysis does not capture all the information about time-related outcomes during the period of the study. In particular, the approach adopted emphasises outflows from unemployment, but does not consider flows back into unemployment. Restart might reduce the time to exit from unemployment, but if the time to return to unemployment is also correspondingly reduced, then the net reduction in time as an unemployed claimant will be zero. We need a measure which reflects the effects of back-flows as well as outflows. A measure which meets this need is the proportion of the study period spent as an unemployed claimant (and, similarly, proportion of time in employment, or in government programmes, or in a non-claimant but non-employed status).

Even this simple measure, however, raised some complications. In particular, there were many individuals who never left unemployment, who never entered a job, who never entered a programme, and so on. When values cluster like this at some artificial limiting value, in this case either 100 per cent or 0 per cent, the ordinary regression estimates tend to be invalid. It is possible to circumvent this problem by using the method of censored regression analysis,[14] which provides consistent and efficient estimates. The price paid for this is a loss of transparency: the estimates can no longer be interpreted in the same way as the estimates from ordinary regression analysis.

In a few instances, the outcome measure we used related to individuals' situation at a particular point in time. For example, for some purposes we looked at whether or not each person was unemployed at the time of the Restart interview, or a month after the Restart interview, or at the first survey interview. This kind of outcome can be analysed by non-linear regression analysis (logistic regression). Its chief limitations are that many such 'snapshots' would have to be taken to give a fair picture of the whole study period; and, at any one point in time, those with relatively long periods in the unemployed (or other) status are over-represented relative to those with short periods. This type of outcome measure is useful chiefly where the point in time which is considered is of inherent interest (for example, we want to know what happens soon after the Restart interview).

So, while no one measure tells the whole story, by using these types of measure in combination, we believe that a balanced view of outcomes is obtained. In addition, we make quite extensive use of *ad hoc* descriptive analyses to give a better insight into the workings of Restart. These require no general introduction, and will be explained as they are brought into later chapters.

Multivariate modelling
In principle, a survey design incorporating a random control group should make it possible to assess the effects of a programme in rather a simple way. There should be no systematic differences between the control group and the programme group (as the tests described above have confirmed), and differences between the two groups on outcome measures should be directly testable without the need to take account of compositional differences.

In practice, however, it remains advantageous to retain background variables in the analysis and adopt a multivariate approach. Partly this is simply a failsafe precaution against the existence of any bias in the composition of the control group, with respect to any of the outcomes of interest. Controlling for a wide range of the variables known, from previous research, to influence labour market outcomes increases confidence that any differences found between the control group and the programme group are genuine.

One source of bias present in most surveys is non-response. Those who cannot be contacted, or refuse to take part in survey interviews, may well be different in other characteristics from those who do take part. Controlling for a wide range of variables would tend to reduce any bias from this source. In recent years, moreover, statistical techniques have been developed which directly address the situation where part of the sample is missing or 'selected out'. Provided that sufficient information is available to model this prior selection as a first stage, the analysis of the remaining sample can be adjusted statistically as a second stage to allow for the displacement resulting from the absent section of data.[15] The technique, often referred to as sample selection modelling, has been used in this research to assess the non-response problem, and it requires a framework of multivariate analysis to be applied.

One of the main reasons for using a multivariate approach is a presentational one: it is to interpret the size of the effect of Restart upon outcomes, if any. By placing the estimated Restart effect alongside estimates of other effects upon outcomes, from factors such as age, gender and education, all of which have been obtained in a combined analysis, a good sense of the practical importance of Restart can be gained. This is particularly useful here because, with a relatively small control group, effects of Restart cannot be estimated with a high degree of numerical precision.

Selection of variables for modelling

It was not necessary for this study to develop the most complete or sophisticated models of unemployment outcomes: logically, and on the basis of experience,[16] control group designs should produce estimates which are little affected by the presence or absence of other variables. On the other hand we wanted to include a sufficiently wide range of variables to provide us with insurance against bias in our assessment of the Restart effects, and with useful comparators for interpreting the size of those effects. At the same time we did not want extremely large models which might divert resources from the aims of the study.

The approach adopted to find a compromise was to have an exploratory stage of the study, in which a wide range of variables was tested. The outcomes examined at this stage were confined for the most part to binary variables (logistic regression models). Through this exploratory process, variables were dropped from the analyses if (a) they never showed significant relationships with the outcome measures, or (b) the relationships which they displayed were of lower magnitude than those of closely similar alternative variables, or (c) they created technical problems in the analyses, e.g. due to collinearity with other variables. The variables retained after this process were used as a 'standard' set for most of the multivariate analyses presented in this report.

The retained and dropped variables can usefully be summarised under several headings (the short label attached to each retained variable permits further details to be retrieved from the archived survey documentation and dataset).

(a) Local labour market variables. Those retained were as follows:

• DUN8890 – Change in unemployment, 1988-90: this variable was calculated from NOMIS travel-to-work area data and reflected the difference in the four-quarter average for 1990 relative to the similar statistic in 1988. It therefore measured improvement in local labour market conditions over the time of the claim and the study.

• FPS89 – Local labour market turnover, 1989: this was another variable calculated from NOMIS data, and was based on the four-quarter average of outflow divided by the stock. 1989 was selected as the mid-year of the study period.

• IC – Inner city area: an Employment Service classification of employment office areas as either 'inner city' or not provided a binary variable.

Other variables tested but not used were drawn from the NOMIS database. These included absolute (rate) measures of unemployment in 1988, 1989 and 1990, and the 1988-89 and 1989-90 difference measures. None of these performed as well as the 1988-90 difference measure.

(b) Short-term economic variable. Linearly changing economic conditions during the period of the study were controlled by including: SWEEK – the start-week of the individual's unemployment claim, counted as 1 to 18 over the sampling period of four months. (Later entrants to the survey received both Restart interviews and survey interviews at a later point, so that their experience is likely to reflect slightly worsening conditions as recession began to develop during late 1989-early 1990.)

No alternative variable was tried under this heading.

(c) Human capital variables. Those retained were as follows:

- AQ – Any educational qualification (from Certificate of School Education upward), a binary variable

- TQ – Any technical or vocational qualification (from Part I City & Guilds upwards), a binary variable

(Both the above were derived from the standard question on qualifications used in the General Household Survey.)

- DVLY – Current driving licence held, a binary variable

- JPC3 – Percentage of time spent in employment or self-employment during 1985-87, netting out time spent on government programmes or in full-time education.

Variables tested but dropped included: O-level qualification, A-level qualification, time spent in government programmes in preceding years, and the five-year (1984-88) version of JPC.

(d) Occupational level. No variable was retained under this heading. The variables tested were all based upon the Goldthorpe classes schema, with an additional category for those 'never employed', and related to: the most recent job before the current claim, or the 'most representative' job in the whole prior employment. The lack of association with outcome variables probably reflects in part the concentration of much of the sample in lower occupations, and in part the overriding effects of human capital variables and age, both of which are associated with occupational level.

(e) Claimant history. One variable only was tried under this heading, as it appeared extremely effective:

- MOPC – Months claiming as unemployed during the period 1982-87, expressed as a percentage of the months in this period that the individual was aged 16 or over. In some analyses, MOPC proved to be collinear with JPC3 so that only one could be used. Months claiming in 1988 prior to the current unemployment spell were not included in this measure, as we did not want it to be too closely connected with that current spell.

(f) Other characteristics. The following characteristics, all of which are widely used in analyses of unemployment, were included:

• FEM – Gender of individual, coded 1 if female and 0 if male

• AGEG – Age, banded into five groups to conform with the usual conventions of published statistics: less than 25, 25-34, 35-44, 45-54, 55 or over. A banded variable rather than a continuous age variable was used since in some cases the age effect is non-linear or 'kinked'.

• MARY – Marital status, with three categories: married or living with partner, divorced/separated/widowed, single.

• DKID – the number of dependent children.

• TODL – the number of children aged under five, taken as a three-category variable: none, one, two or more.

• ETH – ethnic origin, usually taken as having four categories: white, Afro-caribbean, Indian or Pakistani, and other.

• HTHY – self-report as having a disability or problem of ill-health which limits the type of work which can be done; a binary variable.

• LARY – householder in local authority rented accommodation, a binary variable.

Other variables tested but dropped under this heading included: two other indicators of previous health problems; number of people in household; type of housing; whether head of household or not; whether living independently or with parents; amount of benefits currently received (the benefits data from this survey were somewhat limited, and number of children probably acts as a reasonable proxy).

(g) Job search. Although not always incorporated, job search was used as a mediating variable in some analyses. The measure selected to represent this was:

• A4G – the frequency of job applications, in a reference period of four weeks, classified in five bands: none, 1-4, 5-9, 10-19, 20 or more.

The main alternative tested was whether the individual had ceased seeking for work for a period of six months (a binary variable). This distinguished only a small group within the sample and gave rise to problems of logical dependency with outcome variables.

(h) Other intervening variables. Various other variables which might be regarded as intervening between personal and background characteristics on one hand, and outcomes on the other, were captured by the survey: for example, receiving various forms of help from services at employment offices, and their reported perceptions or responses to those services. In general, however, exploratory analyses showed that these had either non-significant relations with outcomes or, where significant, had the opposite signs to what would be intuitively expected. It seems likely that such variables are subject to a degree of self-selection bias, at least in this survey, and cannot safely be used as intervening variables.

Unobserved variables. It is worth noting that those models using an outcome measure based on an over-time difference, implicitly control to some extent for unobserved variables which persist over time. For example, unobserved motivational variables which were at the same level both in the 'before' period and the 'after' period would be eliminated by the differencing method. With a control group design, unobserved variables in any case should not pose a substantial problem (unlike in the case of a nonexperimental comparison group design), because their presence in the control group is random.

Model specifications

Since both the form of the outcome variables, and the selection of explanatory variables, have been described in previous sections, it remains only to outline the general approach to specification of the multivariate models.

Because of the control group design, it was not necessary to model participation in the Restart programme as a preliminary step to modelling its effects. Restart effects could generally be obtained with a one-stage estimation procedure (the main exception being where we considered the potential effects of non-response).

The approach was usually to seek the simplest possible form of the model consistent with not doing violence to the data. In most cases, for example, we made no attempt to introduce interactions between explanatory variables into the models. We expressed the model in an additive or 'main effects' form, that is, the effect of each variable is averaged across the values of the other variables.

This applied, most importantly, to the Restart variable itself: in most cases, we did not consider the possibility that the Restart effect varied for different categories within the population. Though it would have been of value to consider such differential effects, the relatively small size of the control group acted as a practical constraint. As we subdivide the control group, we obtain estimates of rapidly decreasing precision.

For the same reason, we did not (as many labour market analysts do) routinely estimate separate models for male and female sub-samples throughout, nor did we do so for different age-groups. We did, however, at a few points where differences were expected on good *a priori* grounds estimate separately for men and women. We did, also, carry out a limited test of whether Restart effects might differ by gender or by age-group, using the full sample (including non-respondents) and hence having the largest possible control group. These tests, reported in Chapter 4, indicated (as far as they went) that there were not significant differences in Restart effects by gender or age; and if not in the case of these, the chief variables of unemployment, it seems reasonably unlikely that interactions existed elsewhere. That, however, has to remain a surmise.

Finally, a few technicalities may be worth noting.

(a) In estimating the two-stage sample selection models, we used the maximum likelihood estimation method rather than the Heckman method.[17]

(b) In the case of the survival analyses, we used parametric models. The use of parametric models raises questions about the form of the underlying distribution of survival times which is to be assumed. Closely connected with this is an issue, widely discussed among labour market analysts, as to whether there exists 'duration dependence' in outcomes such as exits from unemployment or entry to jobs. By duration dependence is meant, roughly speaking, that the probability of the outcome tends to change as time goes on; it may become either more probable or less probable after a longer period in the present state. An example of this is the frequently expressed view that as people remain longer in unemployment, employers become less willing to consider them seriously as job applicants.

Some analysts use a Weibull distribution assumption and interpret the time parameter in the model as indicating duration dependence if it is substantially different from one. This however is debatable; duration dependence cannot be demonstrated in longitudinal data except on the basis of prior distributional assumptions,[18] which should be independently justified if the inferences are not to involve a degree of circularity. Since the issue of duration dependence is not of concern to our inquiry, we generally preferred to make the 'null assumption' of no duration dependence and hence to assume that the underlying distribution was exponential.[19] We have, however, carried out parallel analyses with Weibull distribution assumptions so that the sensitivity of the findings to our distribution assumptions could be tested. We do find that in some analyses, the time parameter is considerably different from one, and a Weibull distribution assumption appears to be supported against an exponential distribution assumption.[20] On the other hand, where we have most complete data, the results are closely consistent with the exponential distribution assumption. For the reasons already stated, we do not consider the apparent departures from the exponential distribution as strong evidence of duration dependence. What is more important, for the objectives of the present study, is that the estimated Restart effects in these analyses are mostly not much affected by whether one uses an exponential or a Weibull distribution assumption. We chiefly focus on the results with exponential distribution assumptions, but some details of the parallel analyses with Weibull assumptions are provided in the notes.

(c) Because this was a stratified sample with variable sampling fractions, it was necessary to incorporate a corrective weight in the multivariate analyses. This weighting does not affect the sample size on which statistical tests are based. Its effect is to increase the variance and so reduce the precision of estimates. Tables have also been weighted in most cases; exceptions are explained in the text.

In conclusion, it should be recalled that the focus of this study is not upon the development of new and better general models of unemployment or of exits from unemployment. Our aim is to assess the effects of Restart. With that aim in mind, we have sought to keep the model specifications and assumptions reasonably straightforward.

Statistical evaluation of Restart effects

The chief task of the analysis has been taken to be the assessment of the significance of Restart effects. It seemed reasonable to hypothesize that Restart should reduce the time taken to exit from unemployment, and the proportion of time spent in unemployment. Similarly, it should reduce the time taken to enter employment (including self-employment), to enter ET or other government programmes, and to enter a non-employed, non-claimant status. It should increase the proportion of time spent in employment, ET and other programmes, and non-claimant status. Restart might also be hypothesized to increase job-search. Since we are able to hypothesize the direction of Restart effects in all these cases, it is appropriate to apply a one-tailed significance test to the estimates of Restart effects. In the case of wage variables (actual wages, target wages or reservation wages), the direction of the effect is hard to predict since Restart could involve contrary influences, so that a two-tailed test would appear appropriate in these cases.

It should be appreciated that the Restart effects are assessed in this research through quite a wide range of analyses. With many analyses being performed, results may be obtained in a particular case which appear significant but actually reflect the operation of chance. Conversely, identifying results which are individually significant in numerous conceptually related analyses, according to some views of statistical inference, increases the reliability of the findings above the level indicated by any single analysis within the set.

Because of the relatively small size of the control group, the estimates of the Restart effect (which are based on comparisons of those entering Restart with those in the control group) are likely to be relatively imprecise – that is, to have quite wide confidence intervals attached to them.

Graphical presentation

We have only in a few instances been able to apply the familiar ordinary least squares regression approach, with its easily interpretable estimates: most of the analyses involve non-linear estimation. This raises a problem of presentation. We have followed an increasingly common practice with such estimates, of presenting them in a graphical form, with each effect represented as a bar. It is hoped that this type of chart will make it easier for the reader to see the estimates of effects in a comparative way.

The first step in constructing such a figure is to calculate the value of the dependent variable for a 'base case' individual who is defined by a set of values on all the variables in the estimation model. This value of the outcome is represented by a bar. Then each other bar of the chart represents the effect of re-calculating the value of the dependent variable by changing the value of a *single* explanatory variable.

In the case of censored regression models, the calculations involved use of a computer program, for the use of which we are indebted to Clive Payne.

2   The Labour Market Background and Sample Characteristics

The Restart programme, which this study was designed to evaluate, was developed in a decade of remarkable change in the British labour market. Although the conditions under which Restart was launched may be familiar to readers of this report, it may nevertheless be useful to provide a brief sketch of the background. The reasons for doing so are three:

1   This background has to be considered in a direct way in order to arrive at a full understanding of the effects of the Restart process.

2   The background also helps to explain the great increase in interest in labour market measures such as Restart.

3   Although much of the background may currently be familiar, it may not be within the span of a few years as new conditions may emerge. Those referring to the report after some interval could be misled by the results unless they view them in context.

The second part of the chapter provides some descriptive information about characteristics of the sample used for the study. As with the labour market background, the purpose of this section is to provide background information which is helpful in understanding the task facing the Restart system, and in interpreting the results of the study. There is a likely connection between the labour market conditions of recent years, and the characteristics of people in unemployment at the time of the study.

Unemployment and employment
With the benefit of hindsight, it is now clear that the increases in unemployment experienced in the 1980s resulted in part from economic conditions which began to make themselves felt at least two decades previously. The post-war period of sustained low

unemployment in Britain was, in the mid-1960s, under severe pressure from wage-inflationary tendencies and from worsening trade balances. By the late 1960s, the first substantial rise in unemployment was taking place. This rise could not be interpreted as wholly cyclical, because in the following period of recovery, unemployment did not fall to its previous level. A pattern had thus commenced, which was to continue until the end of the 1980s.

Successive economic crises, originating in externally created crises (such as the USA's withdrawal of dollar convertibility or the 1973 and 1979 oil shocks), resulted in sharp increases in unemployment. Since on each occasion the subsequent fall of unemployment was incomplete, the overall result was one of a *cumulatively rising level of aggregate unemployment*. The early increases were relatively small in absolute terms, but their size grew as time went on. Figure 2.1 shows this development.

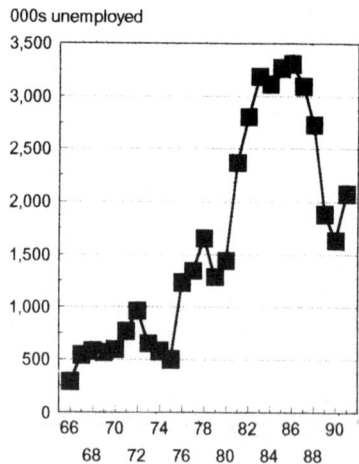

Fig. 2.1   Aggregate unemployment in Great Britain, 1966-91

Source: Department of Employment Gazette and Employment Gazette, statistical series: April of each year

Note: Changes in the definition of unemployment mean that aggregate statistics cannot be compared over the long term in a precise sense

Although the rise in aggregate unemployment of the 1980s could be seen as continuation of the earlier change, it also aggravated it in an important way. Not only was recovery incomplete, but it was greatly delayed. An economic recession of about two years (1980-81) was associated with an unusually high level of unemployment which persisted for seven years.

This *persistence* of unemployment, which was experienced in a number of the other large advanced economies at about the same time,[1] was completely unexpected. It has provided one of the focal points of recent economic investigations and explanations. It is worth stressing that this persistence of unemployment in the presence of macroeconomic 'boom' conditions is unprecedented in British economic history. The existence of this problem was highly germane to Restart, which was piloted and then launched nationally in 1986. Indeed, Restart can in part be viewed as a specific response (not, of course, the sole response) to this unique problem.

This brief resumé has identified three important observations concerning the level of aggregate unemployment which stand in need of explanation:

a. the change from a long period of consistently low unemployment to an equally long period of rising and high unemployment;

b. the incomplete recoveries in the economic cycles of the latter period;

c. the full emergence of persistent high unemployment during the 1980s.

A contextual macroeconomic variable of particular interest is aggregate *employment*. The general picture in the UK, over the post-war period as a whole, has been one of slow growth in this respect. Between 1951 and 1966, employment rose by 1.5 million, a rate of increase of the order of 0.4 per cent per annum. In the stagnation of the 1970s, employment first contracted (falling as much as 0.7 million below the 1966 peak) but by 1979 had recovered and reached a new peak. During 1979-1982, there was a substantial fall in aggregate employment, cancelling the increases of the entire period since 1950, but by 1983 growth had resumed at a slow pace. There were then wholly exceptional increases during 1988 and 1989, at the time when Restart became a nationally established system. As a result, by 1990 the level of employment was about three per cent higher than at the pre-recession peak of 1979 and average employment growth during the 1980s was as great as in the earlier period.

Restart was, up to the time of our study, designed chiefly as a measure related to *long-term* unemployment, so it is necessary to look also at how this aspect of unemployment has developed. Long-term unemployment is often defined as a continuous period of unemployment of at least one year (although any such definition is to some degree arbitrary); Restart has been first applied after six months of unemployment. During the period of low unemployment prior to 1970, the proportion at any time who were unemployed for as long as one year rarely rose as high as 20 per cent of all unemployment. During the 1970s, unemployment durations began to rise, at first without any apparent relationship to aggregate unemployment, but towards the end of the decade in association with rising unemployment. By 1980 the proportion of long-term unemployed had risen to about 25 per cent, by 1985 to about 40 per cent; with the eventual recovery, it fell back, by the end of 1990, to 30 per cent. The 1980s, with high and persistent unemployment, was also a decade of persistent long-term unemployment.

Analytically, aggregate unemployment, a stock, represents the cumulative balance between rates of inflow and outflow; it changes continuously as a result of these flows. This point is central to an understanding of how a system such as Restart can, in principle, reduce the level of unemployment (and of long-term unemployment) by speeding-up processes of transition. There is a popular tendency, in the UK, to equate unemployment with 'job loss', but it is possible that an increased rate of job loss, if balanced by an increased rate of outflow from unemployment, should result in no net increase in unemployment. Similarly, the average duration of unemployment is (at equilibrium) equal to the stock of unemployed divided by the outflow rate per unit of time. In general, an increasing average duration of unemployment reflects the fact that the outflow rate is either increasing less rapidly or decreasing more slowly, relative to the inflow rate. An increasing aggregate level of unemployment can result either from increasing inflow to unemployment, or from increasing average duration of unemployment, or both.

In the UK, adequate data on unemployment flows only became available in the early 1980s.[2] The great rise in unemployment of the early 1980s can be decomposed into, on one hand, an increased inflow to unemployment, and on the other hand, an increased average duration (or reduced outflow relative to the unemployment level).

Specifically, the duration of male unemployment increased (on average) by more than one half during the period 1978-82, while the inflow of men to unemployment increased by about one-third. In the case of women, the inflow to unemployment increased at a higher rate than the average duration of unemployment, but it was still the case that both components increased considerably. UK unemployment cannot be understood without considering both the acceleration of the inflow and the obstruction of the outflow. Moreover, 'long-term unemployment' should not be seen as a separate 'compartment' within unemployment, when changes in average duration of unemployment are so fundamental to the growth of unemployment in the aggregate.

The implications of persistent unemployment
In the brief sketch of unemployment which we have given, one aspect appears to be of special importance. The persistence of unemployment, through a period of economic boom, was as we have stated the newest feature of the labour market of the 1980s. It stimulated much fresh thinking among labour market specialists to account for the altered conditions. Although this is not the place for a review of such explanations,[3] one is particularly germane to Restart and to the present study. This is the, unfortunately named, hysteresis theory of unemployment. According to this theory, once a situation of high unemployment has been reached (through, for example, the impact of external shocks on the economy), the labour market switches into a new mode of operation. Although particular macroeconomic conditions brought about the high unemployment, reversing these macroeconomic conditions does not have the opposite effect, because one is no longer dealing with the same kind of labour market as before. From a policy viewpoint, it is essential to understand the specific changes which result from high unemployment and lead to unemployment then becoming intractable, and proceed directly to the treatment of those changes, rather than relying upon macroeconomic policies.

Various ideas have been put forward about the nature of the changes which tend to take place as a result of a move into high unemployment. These include: deterioration of the skills and work habits of people who have been affected by lengthy or recurrent unemployment; diminishing effectiveness of financial incentives to work or to search for jobs, as unemployed people become accustomed to a reduced standard of living; and the growing use by employers of unemployment as a recruitment filter, leading to widespread discrimination. More generally, one might say that high unemployment causes damage to the labour market; it is necessary to repair this damage in order to restore its responsiveness to macro-economic influences.[4]

Another closely related notion is that the chances of returning to employment after unemployment are not evenly distributed among unemployed people, but are graded according to such aspects as qualifications and, especially, the length of time that the individual has already been employed. In the recovery phase following a deep recession, therefore, it is those who have had the shortest spells of unemployment, and whose 'human capital' has deteriorated least, who tend to be the first to benefit by getting jobs. As more of these move into employment, those left in long-term unemployment become increasingly clearly identified as a disadvantaged group, and this may accentuate employers' discrimination against them.

It is possible to see a number of the labour market programmes and policies introduced in recent years by governments (in other countries as well as in Britain) as relevant to this kind of analysis. Among these one can certainly place Restart. By enforcing a regular periodic review of each unemployed person's case, Restart is in a position to ensure that individuals do not drift into long-term unemployment by default. This discipline should lead to increased average levels of job search and hene contribute to the functioning of competitive processes in the job market.

In addition, however, the particular character of Restart in any period also depends upon the other labour market programmes or policies in force. This is because Restart operates as a means of ensuring that individuals are brought into contact with these programmes and policies, and that action is taken to counter the effects of cumulative unemployment by making use of these programmes and policies. By providing a convenient gateway into many programmes or services, Restart should increase the effects of those programmes upon the efficiency of the job market, the maintenance and increase of human capital, and so on.

Because Restart was of obvious relevance to current thinking about the nature of persistent unemployment, economists were ready to attribute to it a significant role in the great reduction of unemployment, and especially of long-term unemployment, which took place in 1988 and 1989. There were, however, numerous other changes taking place in parallel, including on the macroeconomic front a period of expansion led by fiscal policy, and on the labour market front, the introduction of Employment Training. The attribution of a major role to Restart could, therefore, be questioned, and the case for existence of a Restart effect has rested chiefly upon macroeconomic modelling studies.[5]

Changes in employment structures

So far this review has focused upon the aggregate changes in employment and unemployment in the period before and during the introduction of Restart. But other changes were taking place, of a more structural nature, and these also could affect the practical operation of a system such as Restart.

Structural change in industries and occupations has been continuous, in Britain as in other advanced economies, from the beginning of the industrial revolution.[6] Such change was however particularly rapid in the recession of the 1980s, and indeed also in the late 1970s. Most of the contraction of employment taking place in the recession was concentrated (a) in manufacturing industries, and (b) in manual occupations. As growth of employment revived during the 1980s, it was initially concentrated almost wholly in the service industries, and about three quarters of the additional jobs created were in white collar work, especially the higher (professional, technical and managerial) occupations.[7] Although, as already noted, such structural changes were continuations of existing trends, what was new was their conjunction with a period of persistent unemployment. Unemployed people from manufacturing jobs in general proved capable of moving into the growing service industries, but movement from the contracting manual occupations into the growing white-collar occupations proved more difficult, presumably because of the educational barriers between occupations.[8] Accordingly, the unemployment of the 1980s, and especially long-term unemployment, was heavily concentrated among manual workers. Only with the major labour market expansion of 1988 and 1989, was employment in manufacturing stabilised and some new growth for manual employment created.[9]

There were other important compositional shifts in employment during the 1980s. One of the most remarkable features was a revival in self-employment, an area in which the UK previously ranked lowest among all the OECD nations. The proportion of self-employment stood at eight per cent of total employment at the start of the decade, but had risen to 14 per cent at the end. It pre-dated the employment boom of 1988-89 but continued strongly through it. Apart from self-employment, job growth was largely concentrated, initially, in part-time employment and in female employment. Indeed, part-time and female job growth was more rapid than at any time since the start of the 1970s. During 1988-89, however, while female employment continued to expand strongly, the role of part-time jobs diminished and it was full-time female employment which came through most strongly.[10] Recent evidence shows that there was also, in the 1980s, a marked change in the behaviour of mothers returning to work after childbirth, both in a much higher tendency to wish to work, and in a much higher tendency to return to prior full-time employment.[11]

The period when Restart was becoming established was, then, at least superficially a more favourable one for re-absorbing people into jobs than had been the case for several years. Most unemployed people have sought full-time jobs in manual or lower service occupations, and the market for this type of work was much more buoyant in 1988-89 than for a decade. The more favourable climate for self-employment also offered opportunities which would potentially be open to quite a wide range of unemployed people, and the government's Enterprise Allowance Scheme was indeed widely regarded as highly successful in bringing about this kind of movement.

On the other hand, people in unemployment, and especially those with specific disadvantages in competing for jobs, may also have been facing increased competition at this time, especially from the increasing re-entry or retention of women in employment. The underlying longer-term trend towards increases in higher white-collar occupations was not favourable to a pool of lower-skilled manual workers. Further, there was a question as to how many individuals had experienced a decline in their skills, capacities, or motivation during the years of depressed labour markets. The greater such problems, the greater the task which faced Restart.

Some characteristics of the Restart Cohort Study sample
The preceding review pointed out that unemployment was, during the early 1980s, highly concentrated among manual workers. This was not necessarily a feature which would continue without change. Some studies, notably the Department of Employment's inquiry into the London labour market,[12] began to indicate that increasing proportions of people with advanced or higher qualifications, and from higher-skilled backgrounds, may have been entering unemployment by the mid-1980s.

To evaluate the occupational backgrounds of the sample, we used the Goldthorpe class schema.[13] This divides occupations into 11 categories, which can also be collapsed into a three-fold division of 'higher', 'intermediate' and 'lower'. Those interviewed in the survey gave information about recent past jobs, provided that these had been held within the past five years. The resulting classification is shown in Table 2.1 below.

Table 2.1 Proportions of 'recent' jobs in occupational classes

		weighted percentage of total	
1	Service class - Higher	3.0	
2	Service class - Lower	6.9	
'Higher'			9.9
3	Routine non-manual clerical and administrative	8.7	
4	Routine non-manual distributive	3.8	
5	Small proprietors - 1-25 employees	0.7	
6	Small proprietors - no employees	4.8	
7	Farmers and smallholders	0.1	
8	Supervisors of manual workers; low grade technicians	4.1	
'Intermediate'			22.2
9	Skilled manual workers	11.1	
10	Semi and unskilled manual workers	35.6	
11	Agricultural workers	1.4	
'Lower'			47.1
	No recent previous employment	20.0	
Base: all at first survey interview		4,807	

One of the main problems in applying the classification, with the present sample, is the large proportion – one in five – who had no job in the past five years. This includes younger people who had not held a job since entering the labour market. If we count these as having (implicitly) a lower level of occupation, then the collapsed breakdown becomes: higher occupations, 10 per cent, intermediate occupations, 22 per cent, lower occupations, 68 per cent. If we exclude those without a recent prior occupation from the calculation, then the breakdown becomes: higher occupations, 12 per cent, intermediate occupations, 28 per cent, lower occupations, 60 per cent. The proportion in lower occupations would be substantially increased if we applied an alternative scheme, favoured by some researchers, in which females in categories 3 and 4 are counted as equivalent to semi-skilled manual workers, because their work is (on average) more routine and lower paid than those of men in these categories.

Irrespective of such details, the overall picture is fairly clear. The higher occupations are greatly under-represented, relative to employment proportions, the intermediate occupations are represented roughly in line with employment proportions, while the lower occupations are greatly over-represented.[14] There may have been some shift towards more people from higher-level and intermediate-level occupations entering long-term unemployment, but if so it has not been a large enough shift to be confirmed without further, rather detailed investigation. In broad terms, the picture appears to be much as found in previous studies.[15]

The most important question to be answered about the characteristics of those entering the Restart process, as the discussion of the preceding section makes clear, is the extent to which they have been affected by persistent unemployment. Although the sample consisted of people who, in early 1989, were reaching six months of unemployment, this measure applies to their *current claim*, and does not take account of prior unemployment. Previous research has shown that there is a tendency for unemployment to be followed by rather insecure employment, often leading to further unemployment.[16]

As the survey was able to make use of the JUVOS Cohort database, showing claiming from 1982 onwards, it was possible to calculate the proportions of time spent as an unemployed claimant with a high degree of reliability. In making these calculations, we considered the period 1982-87 inclusive,[17] but excluded from the calculation any part of this period in which the individual was less than 16 years of age and hence still in compulsory schooling.

It was found that the average proportion of time spent as an unemployed claimant, over the six-year period, was 35 per cent or just over one third. This tends to confirm that many people in the sample had experienced persistent unemployment in the preceding years to the study.

From the respondent's recall, we also collected information about the proportion of time spent (a) in employment, and (b) on government training or other labour market programmes, during the three-year period 1985-87.[18] The sample as a whole had spent very close to one half (50 per cent) of its time in employment over this period, and six per cent on government training and other programmes. Once again, the rather low level of average employment indicated the likely presence of labour market disadvantages for many members of the sample.

Two of the most obvious aspects of disadvantage are lack of educational or vocational qualifications, and the presence of disabilities or ill-health.

The people interviewed were shown standard lists of educational and of vocational qualifications,[19] and asked if they possessed any of them. In the sample as a whole,

- 56 per cent had a recognised qualification of some type while 44 per cent lacked any qualification whatever

- 45 per cent had some educational qualification while 55 per cent lacked any educational qualification

- 31 per cent had some vocational qualification while 69 per cent lacked any vocational qualification

- 20 per cent held both an educational and a vocational qualification.

To place this in some perspective, the 1987 General Household survey reported that 66 per cent of all people aged 25-49 had some educational qualification while 34 per cent had no educational qualification whatever.[20] While some additional refinement would be needed to make the figures strictly comparable, there is little doubt that the unemployed sample had a lower educational qualification level than the general population, but it is also apparent that this difference was not great, especially if one took occupational background into account.

In addition, 50 per cent of the sample held a current driving licence, a type of 'qualification' which may be of considerable practical importance on the job market.[21] Data from the 1980 General Household Survey showed that of those aged 21-29, 56 per cent held a driving licence, and this figure would rise to 60 per cent after re-weighting to the proportions of men and women found in the present survey. Precise comparisons would again require more up-to-date information as well as corrections for the age and ocupational structures; probably, the difference between the present sample and the comparable population group was at most a small one.

The reported existence of disabilities or problems of ill-health, believed by the person to have an effect on the type of paid work which could be performed, was one of the most striking descriptive features of the sample. No less than 36 per cent of the sample at the first survey interview reported that they experienced difficulties of this type. Furthermore, when asked at the second survey interview whether they had been affected by any such problems *within the six-month period since the previous survey interview*, 20 per cent affirmed that they had. It can be argued that such reports of disability or ill-health may have low correlation with clinical assessments. But as will become apparent in later chapters, the reports of disability and ill-health were strong predictors of a number of the labour market outcomes which were analysed, and this adds a degree of validity to the reports, even though they are open to various interpretations.

Reports of disability or ill-health were, as would be expected, strongly associated with age. This is shown in Table 2.2 below.

Table 2.2   Disability or ill-health by age group

				column percentages
	Under 25	25-34	35-44	45-54	55+
Report of disability or ill-health (%)	25	30	40	55	55

Base: all at the first survey interview (N=4,807)

The question asked in the survey was not closely comparable with those used in the General Household Survey, which are expressed in terms of limitations on activity in general rather than related to paid work. The figures from the General Household Survey for 1989 are, nevertheless, of some interest.[22] This source showed 21 per cent of unemployed people reporting that they had a long-term limiting illness, a proportion which was nearly twice as high as was the case for people in employment. This result tends to suggest that illness is an important issue in relation to unemployment.

The inflow to unemployment has been, in the past, predominantly a young one.[23] It was not so obvious, however, that an inflow at the stage of six months of unemployment would be youthful, but this proved to be so. As shown in Table 2.3 below, 60 per cent of the sample was under 35 and only 10 per cent over 55.

Table 2.3   Age distribution of the sample

	Under 25	25-34	35-44	45-54	55+
Percent of total	34	27	16	13	10

Base: total sample (N=8,189)

The division of the sample by male and female was much as expected from previous surveys and from national statistics of unemployment, with 68 per cent male and 32 per cent female. The lower proportions of women in unemployment (relative to their share of employment) are generally interpreted as the result of several factors in combination: occupational segregation by gender, and the more plentiful labour market opportunities in 'women's jobs'; lower probability of women having unemployment benefit entitlement; and the availability of traditional domestic roles into which women may tend to withdraw.

The age and gender distributions of the sample also influence a number of other characteristics which may be important for labour market outcomes. It was found that 47 per cent of the sample (based on the first survey interview) were married or had partners, while 43 per cent were single and 10 per cent were divorced, separated or widowed. Only 28 per cent had any dependant children: 14 per cent one child only, nine per cent two children, and five per cent three or more children. However, among those that did have children, there was a high probability that they would be of pre-school age. Some 14 per cent of the sample had a single child under five years of age, and five per cent had two or more children of this age.

Concluding comments

This brief review has pointed to some of the most important features of the labour markets of the 1980s, and has then described some of the main characteristics of the sample used in the present study. Both of these aspects can be seen as part of the context within which Restart had to operate.

Restart began, as a national system, at a time which was in some ways highly favourable, because of the remarkable employment boom which took place in 1988 and 1989 (and to which Restart may itself have contributed from the supply side). On the other hand, the persistent unemployment during the preceding years may also have left behind difficult problems for Restart to cope with. As jobs expand, there may be a tendency for those in unemployment who are better-equipped to be 'creamed off' into jobs while those who remain have, on average, substantial disadvantages. Even if this does not take place, entrants to unemployment have tended to come from lower occupations, with correspondingly low qualifications, and these characteristics may create obstacles to the adjustment of the labour market.[24]

Many individuals in the sample did appear to have a substantial degree of disadvantage in competing for jobs. This was indicated by the large proportions in the sample with low occupational level or no recent previous employment, the high average proportion of time spent claiming during 1982-87, the high prevalence of non-qualification, and the high prevalence of reported disabilities or problems of ill-health.

The Restart system appears, according to some theoretical explanations of persistent unemployment, as an appropriate policy initiative which should, in combination with other programmes, be capable of accelerating flows out of unemployment and (in conjunction with other programmes) contributing to the efficient functioning of a competitive job market. The description of the characteristics of those entering the Restart process after six months of unemployment suggests the constraints or difficulties likely to face such a system. These characteristics of Restart clients may impose practical constraints on its operation, and is likely to influence the particular way in which it carries out its task.

3   The Restart Process

It is better to think of the Restart programme as a process which continues over a period, rather than as a single event. The purpose of this chapter is to describe the Restart process, and to examine some of the possible influences upon its operation. This will provide essential background to the later chapters which consider the effects of the Restart process.

The administrative process
We begin by outlining the Restart process in a formal way, by describing the various steps taken by staff in the local offices (usually Jobcentres) where Restart interviews were held. To construct this outline, we draw upon the detailed description of procedures which staff of the Employment Service compiled to assist in sampling for the study. In addition, two visits were made by members of the PSI team to Restart offices, to observe Restart interviews and associated procedures. It must be understood that the outline refers to administrative procedures in 1989, the time when the study was being carried out (see Chapter 1).

The lists. Restart procedures began with the arrival of a computer generated list of those claimants, at a particular local office, who were approaching an unbroken period of claim of six months. These lists were produced fortnightly, and therefore collected together claimants with a small variation in their period of unemployment. In order to allow enough time for the local offices to organise Restart interviews at or soon after the six-month point in the claim, the lists actually reflected the position at a little after five months of unemployment. This time gap between initial selection of names and the date of the Restart interviews is of considerable importance.

The mailing. Upon receipt of a list, the Restart office carried out a mailing to those identified. A letter was sent, asking the individual to attend for an interview at a stated date and time. The letter made clear that attendance at an interview was obligatory for those continuing their unemployment claim. In addition, a short form or questionnaire was enclosed, which the individual was asked to complete and bring to the interview. The questionnaire was designed to provide a brief review of the job search activities currently being pursued, the type of work for which the person felt they would be suitable, and the person's availability for work. The mailings generally took place about two weeks before the individual was called to the interview.

Between mailing and appointment. The majority of those sent a Restart letter subsequently attended the appointment for their counselling interview, but substantial minorities did not. These need to be considered before we turn to the interview.

a. Some would contact the Restart office and change the date or time of their appointment by agreement. The present study has no information of how numerous these cases were or what the circumstances were. The effect of such a change of appointment may be that the Restart interview is delayed somewhat.

b. Some failed to attend the original appointment, were sent a second letter asking them to attend at another appointment, and eventually attended. Administrative records, linked to the survey data, show that of our sample 18 per cent received a second letter.

c. Some, despite being followed up, never attended a Restart interview and were classified as 'failed to attend'. The proportion in this case was 6.5 per cent of the sample. In these cases, the names would be passed to the Benefit Office for possible investigation or withdrawal of benefits. As we shall see later, however, in many cases those failing to attend already had jobs or were on the way to having jobs, and had merely not informed the local office of this change.

d. A more substantial proportion – 11.6 per cent – were classified as 'excused interview'. These were people who told the Restart office of circumstances which made an interview inappropriate. They may have already obtained a job, or a place on Employment Training or another programme, or withdrawn their unemployment benefits claim, in the lag between being listed for interview and the date of the appointment. They may have told the

Restart office that, although not yet in employment, they already had a job lined up or had good prospects of one.

It can be seen, therefore, that many early exits were taking place at about the same time as the Restart interviews.

The Restart interview. The Restart interviews at this time were carried out by staff devoting all their time to Restart. In most cases, the Restart office was located at a Jobcentre or a Benefit Office, but was a distinct part of it.

Although appointments for interviews were pre-arranged, the Restart counsellors generally had a continuous stream of interviews to manage, and because of variable length, there could be delays. The clients were warned that they might have to wait for their appointments, and all offices provided a waiting area.

The interviews observed in the visits to two offices were generally of 15 to 20 minutes. This agrees well with the administrative data; officers recorded the time of each interview, and the average for the sample was 19.5 minutes. However, there were gaps in the records for this item in five per cent of cases. Few of the Restart interviews were of less than 10 minutes or more than 30 minutes.

Second interviews. Although the majority of clients received one interview, for 18 per cent of the sample a second or follow-up Restart interview was arranged and took place. We have no information about the criteria on the basis of which officers decided to bring an individual back for second interview. However, some circumstantial evidence (which will be presented later) indicates that those coming to second interviews tended to have more problems or to be in a more disadvantageous position. If this is right, then second interviews can be seen as efforts to give additional help to those most in need of it.

Restart actions. The instructions under which local Employment Service staff worked emphasised the necessity of arriving at a definite course of action as a result of the interview. On the administrative record of the interview, the counsellor was obliged to enter which action resulted.

The Restart counsellor chiefly acted indirectly by submitting or referring the client to one of the other parts of the system which had responsibilities for services or programmes. For example, the Restart counsellor could:

• put the client in touch with Jobcentre staff in connection with a job

- send the client to an assessment interview to judge suitability for local Employment Training (ET) provision
- refer the client for possible acceptance into a local Jobclub programme
- send the client for a short Restart Course
- refer the client to a Disablement Resettlement Officer to receive further advice or help in relation to a disability
- refer the client to a Claimant Advisor (located at Benefit Offices) to have their benefit entitlement or claimant status re-evaluated.

Formally, the Restart counsellors recorded the immediate action outcome of the process under one of a variety of headings. These were subsequently amalgamated at Head Office to allocate each individual as far as possible to one of eight categories, shown below. (We have slightly modified some of the labels used internally by the Employment Service, to avoid possible misunderstandings. We will also for the sake of simplicity speak of these categories as being allocated by the Restart counsellors although in reality they were working with more detailed coding).

1 'Placed': into a job, ET, Jobclub, etc.

2 'Submitted' (but not placed): the person was sent forward to a placement, but was not accepted, or the placement did not take effect for some other reason

3 'Referred (to DRO, etc.)': the individual was sent on to a Disablement Resettlement Officer, or other specialist advisory service.

4 'Refused offer – referred for review': an offer of a placement (or of submission to a placement) was refused by the individual, as a result of which the person's claim to benefits was referred for review to a Claimant Advisor, etc.

5 'Refused offer, not referred': the refusal took place as above, but no further action resulted

6 'Offer not appropriate': either no offer was proposed, or an initial placement offer was made but this was subsequently withdrawn (usually because of a change in the individual's circumstances: for example, an individual might fall sick, obtain a job, etc.)

7   'Failed to attend': as previously explained

8   'Excused interview': as previously explained.

In a proportion of cases, none of these codes was allocated and the individual was classified as 'Unknown'. It seems that in many cases these may have been people put forward for placement, but following delays in the system, the outcome of the placement was lost track of.

The distribution of Restart actions is shown in Table 3.1. It can be seen that 10 per cent of Restart interviews directly resulted in a placement, a further 23 per cent resulted in an unsuccessful attempt at placement (the largest single category), and in 21 per cent of cases, the offer of placement was either refused on the side of the client, or became inappropriate because of changing circumstances. Referral for assistance by a DRO, etc., was another major category, resulting from 16 per cent of interviews.

Table 3.1   Restart 'action' categories

	weighted per cent of total
'Placed'	10.3
'Submitted but not placed'	22.7
'Referred (to DRO etc)'	16.2
'Refused offer - referred for review'	1.6
'Refused offer - not referred'	9.4
'Offer not appropriate'	9.7
'Excused interview'	13.0
'Failed to attend'	8.9
Unknown	1.7
Control group	6.5

Base: whole survey including
non-respondents (N=8189)

These figures related only to the short-term outcomes of the Restart interviews, since the paperwork from which the information came had to be completed within at most two months of the interview itself. It would however be possible for the Restart process to lead to longer-term outcomes, and it is with those longer-term outcomes, rather than the immediate actions, that the present study is concerned. For example, placing a person into ET or another programme could affect that individual's chances of getting a job some months further on. Similarly, even an unsuccessful submission to placement could stimulate the individual's job search efforts and result in increased chances of employment; or the reverse, through disappointment and reduction of job search.

Other routes through the system

The outline just sketched indicates that the Restart interview is an important gateway or entry-point into many other parts of the system of services for unemployment. For example, Restart counsellors constituted one of the main referral points into ET, especially as the timing of the Restart interview (at six monthly intervals) matched time-related criteria for entry to ET.[1]

It is important, however, not to exaggerate the role of the Restart process in the wider system, which is a complex one. Though Restart can be thought of as a gateway, there are numerous other gateways. So far as job vacancies are concerned, in particular, Restart should not be expected to have a prominent role. The people coming to these Restart interviews have already had six months of unemployment, in which they will have become familiar with the services available at Jobcentres. Indeed, they may already have exhausted many of the more obvious possibilities for finding a job, and will perhaps by this time need different kinds of help. In the case of ET, Restart is by no means the only channel of entry. Individuals can be referred by the general Jobcentre staff, and many apply direct to ET managing agents or providers.

It is important to appreciate that this is the case, in order to understand the position of the control group in the present study. Although not involved in the Restart process, members of the control group still had access to all the other channels within the system. They were not excluded from ET, Jobclubs, Restart courses, and so on. They would, of course, be making use of general Jobcentre services in a perfectly normal way.

The Restart process, then, did not uniquely control access to help and resources. It did not so much modify the system of services as provide an over-laying structure. Its aim was to make the system work better. The evaluation study, therefore, is not directly concerned with the performance of ET, Jobclubs and so on, which would be there with or without Restart. It is concerned with how successful Restart has been in 'adding value' to the operation of the system.

Restart through the eyes of its clients
For details of the operation of Restart, we turn to information from the survey interviews. A quite extensive series of questions about the individuals' experience of Restart, and associated parts of the system, was asked in each stage of the survey. To cover all of this material in detail would divert us too far from the main aim of the study. It is, however, important for an eventual interpretation of Restart effects to know how it is seen by clients. We therefore selectively present the chief points from this section of the survey.

In doing so, we will confine ourselves to results from the first survey interview. These are the most relevant to our purpose, since it is at this stage that the control group members are most clearly distinguished from those passing through Restart (see Chapter 1). In addition, we have a larger sample both in total and, still more, in terms of those having a current unemployment claim. By the time of the second interview, many people had moved off the register and so questions about the Restart process were less widely applicable.

Problems of recall. When considering these results, it is important to bear in mind the timing of the survey interviews. These occurred, on average, some five months after the Restart interviews to which the questions referred. If the main aim of the survey had been to gain individuals' perceptions of the Restart process, it would have been much better to reduce this gap, which must have put a strain on some people's memories. As we examine the results, the existence of problems of recall will become apparent.

The Restart letter. After excluding the control group, some 91 per cent of the Restart Cohort Study sample at the first survey interview recalled receiving a Restart letter. It seems, then, that nearly 10 per cent of those who should have received a letter did not get one or, much more probably, that they had forgotten receiving one after a lapse of some months.

If recall of the letter is tabulated by Restart action group, a quite revealing difference emerges (Table 3.2).

Table 3.2   Recall of the Restart letter

Restart action group	% recalling letter
Placed	93
Submitted, not placed	95
Referred (to DRO, etc.)	95
Declined offer & referred	97
Declined offer - not referred	96
Offer not appropriate	94
Excused interview	75
Failed to attend	84

Base: all at first survey interview
excluding control group (N=4,567)

The two groups with particularly low recall of receiving a letter were those who had made an early exit from the whole Restart process: those who failed to attend interview, and (especially) those who were excused interview. Part of the reason for failing to remember, in these cases, may be that the letter did not begin a wider Restart process. Further, we will later show that these early exits from Restart contain the highest proportion going into jobs. In these cases, the impression made by the letter might well have been erased by the more salient experience of getting back to employment shortly after.

A further analysis (not shown here) looked directly at the connection between remembering the Restart letter and being in a job at an early stage (by the end of the month in which the individual was sampled). This showed that, as expected, entering a job at an early point made people less likely to remember the letter. A similar analysis considered moving off the register at an early stage, for any reason (job or other). In this case, the differences in recall of the letter were very small between those moving off the register early and the remainder. It does seem, therefore, that it is specifically the experience of moving into a job which tends to erase memory of the Restart letter.

A further survey question asked whether receiving the letter had led its recipients to take any action, and, specifically, whether they had increased their search for a job. Some 11 per cent of the sample felt the letter had led to some action, and in nearly eight per cent of cases, this consisted of increased job search. It might occasion some surprise that merely the receipt of a letter should lead to an increase in job search. But research in other fields has shown that focusing of attention can have a significant effect on behaviour. Furthermore, the proportions reporting this influence of the Restart letter varied across the Restart action groups in a plausible way, as Table 3.3 shows.

Table 3.3   Increased job search after Restart letter

Restart action group	% reporting increased job search after letter
Placed	13
Submitted, not placed	11
Referred (to DRO, etc.)	8
Declined offer & referred	5
Declined offer - not referred	5
Offer not appropriate	4
Excused interview	3
Failed to attend	9

Base: all at first survey interview
except control group (N=4,567)

It seems, then, that an early positive reaction to the letter may have been associated, at least to a small degree, with subsequently being placed or submitted for placement through Restart. But interpretation is made difficult by the possibility of selective memory (for example, those 'doing best' out of Restart may have remembered most influence).

Most of those (94 per cent) who should have had a Restart interview recalled having one. However, some of those who should not have had a Restart interview also reported having one: 44 per cent of those recorded as 'failing to attend' and 20 per cent of those 'excused interview'. The explanation in these cases is probably that they thought of other kinds of interview which they had had at the time, perhaps with Claimant Advisors or with general staff in the Jobcentre or Benefit Office.

Helpfulness of the Restart interview. Those having interviews were asked how helpful they were. Some 38 per cent of the total sample (or 46 per cent of those whom we can reasonably suppose to have had an interview) thought that it was positively helpful, with most of the remainder thinking that it had made no difference one way or the other. The opinion that the interview had been helpful was strongly related to the Restart action group, as Table 3.4 shows. The first three types of interview outcomes ('placed', 'submitted', or 'referred') were those where clients generally found the interviews helpful, and this seems reasonable.

Partial support for this view comes from another question, asking clients whether the Restart interview had increased their self-confidence. Overall, 18 per cent of those interviewed said that it had, and the positive reply was strongly associated with being 'placed' and also, to a lesser extent, with being 'submitted' (see last column of Table 3.4).

Table 3.4 Clients' opinions of the value of a Restart interview

percentages of action group

Restart action group	% rating interview helpful	% feeling interview raised self-confidence
Placed	58	25
Submitted, not placed	49	19
Referred (to DRO, etc.)	47	13
Declined offer & referred	36	13
Declined offer - not referred	39	11
Offer not appropriate	39	10

The substance of Restart interviews. Numerous questions were posed to the survey sample concerning the topics which had been discussed in their Restart interviews. It was found that most of those who had had a Restart interview recalled several topics which had been discussed. Statistical investigations showed that these topics were not independent of one another, but tended to come in various combinations.[2] We hoped to be able to reduce the substance to a few major 'patterns', but this proved to be unhelpful: too many combinations were present. Accordingly, we will simply describe each topic one by one, but it must be borne in mind that, in practice, each was taken up in combination with one or more of the other topics.

A first view of the substance of the Restart interviews is provided by Table 3.5.

Table 3.5 Frequency of topics in Restart interviews

Topic	% of Restart interviews where topic was discussed
Jobs/vacancies	22
Referral to DRO or ERC	5
Employment Training	51
EAS / starting a business	26
Restart course	19
Base: those recalling participation in a Restart interview (N=4,111)	

Much the most widely discussed possibility was ET, which was recalled as a topic of one half of all interviews. Three other topics (Enterprise Allowance Scheme, jobs or vacancies, and Restart courses) were recalled as topics of around one in four or one in five of interviews. Referral to a Disablement Resettlement Officer or to an Employment Rehabilitation Centre was mentioned as a topic of relatively few interviews (five per cent).

The survey interview also asked two questions in a more general form: whether membership of a Jobclub had been suggested within the past six months, and what proportion had been seen by a Claimant Adviser during the same period. Many, but not all, of these developments would have arisen through the Restart process. The total proportion was 27 per cent in the case of Job Clubs and 17 per cent in the case of interviews with the Claimant Adviser.

How do the topics discussed relate to the classification of Restart participants in terms of action outcomes? The chief features can be quite simply summarised. The 'submitted not placed' group emerged as having the highest overall proportion recalling the discussion of these topics in the Restart interview. The 'placed' and (to a lesser extent) 'referred' groups also had high proportions of topics mentioned, by comparison with the other groups. So the groups which reported the most positive impressions of Restart interviews were the same as those recalling the most topics. The main indicators are summarised in Table 3.6.

Table 3.6   Frequency of topics by Restart categories

% of Restart interviews where topic was discussed

Topic	Placed	Submitted	Referred
Jobs/vacancies	14	31	16
Employment Training	63	52	38
EAS	24	28	29
Restart course	18	23	12

	Refused offer, not referred	Refused offer, referred	Offer not appropriate
Jobs/vacancies	18	22	13
Employment Training	44	32	30
EAS	17	10	16
Restart course	14	17	13

Base: those recalling participation
in a Restart interview (N=4,111)

As well as talking about particular pathways along which clients may travel, counsellors also sometimes discuss more general issues, for example methods of job-seeking. In fact 12 per cent of those having a Restart interview recalled being given advice on how to change their methods of looking for jobs; and the same proportion had been advised to increase the time they spent in job search. The differences between action groups, regarding these topics, were quite small.

Follow-up from Restart interviews. What happens after the Restart interview is more important, in terms of labour market outcomes, than what happens in the interview. Much of what happens, takes place outside Restart itself, which acts as the link or gateway. But in a number of ways, the Restart counsellor can take immediate action. Also, the responsiveness of the individual client to what is discussed in the interview is likely to be important.

Jobs, as shown earlier, were discussed in 22 per cent of Restart interviews. In 13 per cent of all interviews, discussion led to the client agreeing (according to his or her own recall) to apply for a specific job or type of job which the discussion had identified. During or following eight per cent of all interviews, the counsellor contacted a particular employer on behalf of the individual, to inquire about possible jobs.

One half of the interviews focused, in part, upon ET, and according to the respondents, in one half of these cases (one quarter of all interviews) they agreed to apply for an ET place. In the majority of these cases (21 per cent of all interviews) the Restart counsellor made an appointment on behalf of the claimant to be assessed for entry to ET.

In the case of EAS, discussed in one quarter of interviews, some 13 per cent of the interviewed clients agreed to find out more about the possibilities. Following six per cent of interviews, the counsellor made an appointment or inquiry on behalf of the client.

The general picture, then, is that when an important topic was discussed, commitment to some fresh action resulted, on the side of the client, about one half of the time. It should be recalled that several topics were usually discussed in each interview; so this means that, in general, clients left interviews with at least one action to which they were committed, according to their own retrospective accounts. Immediate supportive action (such as making an inquiry on behalf of the client) was taken by the counsellor in about one half of the cases where the client had made a commitment, or roughly one-quarter of all cases of that type. In the remaining cases, presumably, support would have to await contact with another part of the services for unemployed people.

There is one further type of follow-up action from the Restart interview which it is essential to mention. This is the possibility of receiving a further interview, either with the same counsellor or with a different counsellor. These follow-up interviews may be arranged when, for instance, there has not been sufficient time in the first interview to talk through issues or problems. In fact, some 18 per cent of the whole sample, or 23 per cent of those having an initial interview, proceeded to a second interview. Two groups were less likely to have follow-up interviews: those classified as 'offer not appropriate', where the proportion was 18 per cent, and the 'placed' group, where it was only 12 per cent – about half the general level.

Selection into Restart 'actions'

One of the main questions which has been directed at all forms of services for unemployed people, over the years, is how far they are universal in their application and how far they are selective or targeted. The Restart process as a whole is clearly a universal one, applying to all who have reached a period of six months of unemployment. But the preceding sections have shown that those entering the Restart process may diverge in various directions, represented both by the 'actions' in which they are classified and by the contents of their Restart interviews. This internal diversity is consistent with current thinking in the guidance professions, which stresses the need for supporting individual preferences. It raises the question, however, of what underlying differences may exist between those who go in one direction or another. If we can identify such differences, they may help to indicate the nature of the processes of selection, or perhaps of self-selection, which result in differences within Restart.

The method by which this issue was examined involved the use of a multivariate statistical technique. Each Restart 'action' was, in turn, treated as the dependent variable, or variable to be explained, and a standard set of explanatory variables was used for all the analyses.[3] These explanatory variables are very similar to those used in the following chapters, to account for variations in outcomes after Restart (such as time claiming or time in employment). The multivariate analysis permits us to take account of the overlap or association between the explanatory variables, and to test the significance of the relations with each 'action' variable net of this overlap. We can thus screen a large number of potential influences in a more efficient and reliable way than by running numerous cross-tabulations.

It should be stressed, however, that these multivariate analyses do not claim to provide proper explanatory models of how individuals come to be allocated to Restart 'actions'. That could only be done by a study which focused much more closely upon the Restart process itself. Our analyses are, in essence, using statistical methods as a descriptive short-cut, not as a means to full explanation.

The set of explanatory variables which were considered has been discussed in Chapter 1, but for convenience we briefly list them again here:

a. labour market variables: labour turnover (the unemployed flow as a ratio of the unemployed stock) in the local labour market; change in unemployment (the 1990 stock relative to the 1988 stock) in the local labour market; whether or not the local labour market was in an inner city area; the week in which the individual's claim started (representing time-related general economic conditions)

b. personal history: the proportion of time in jobs during the period 1985-87 inclusive

c. personal characteristics including 'human capital': gender; age group; educational qualification (any/none); technical or vocational qualification (any/none); driving licence (yes/no); ethnic group; marital status; number of dependant children; number of children under five; limiting disability or ill-health (yes/no); householder in local authority housing (yes/no).

Although benefit was not included as a separate variable, it should be noted that number of dependant children is the chief factor in variations in benefit entitlement, and is a reliable indicator.

'Placed'. Two personal characteristics were related to whether or not a person was in the 'placed' group in Restart.

i.   Men's odds of being 'placed' were greater than those of women, by an estimated factor of 1.25.[4]

ii. People aged 55 or over, by comparison with those aged less than 25, had odds of being 'placed' which were reduced by a factor of 0.55.

Since ET is one of the main forms of placement accessed through Restart, it is plausible to link these findings to the facts that (i) women are under-represented in ET, relative to their presence in unemployment, and (ii) ET officially excludes people over 50.

It is interesting to note, however, that in other respects there is no indication here of placement through Restart being a 'creaming-off' process. Notably, those with qualifications had no greater odds of being placed than those without, those with more recent job experience had no greater odds than those with less, and those with disability or health problems had no worse odds than those without such problems.

'*Submitted, not placed*'. A remarkable influence on this category was the start-week of the individual's claim: for every week later, the odds of being in this category were multiplied by a factor of 1.05. This may be an artificial result of the survey procedures: when the time comes to make returns, and the outcome of a placement is still not sure, this may be the category which tends to be used. But other interpretations may be possible; for example, there may have been changes in operational policy over the study period, of which we would not be apprised.

Other findings were as follows:

i.   Age acted much as in the case of placement, although the disadvantage for over-55s was less marked.

ii. Those with a single child under five had higher odds of being in this category than others without young children or with more than one young child (the factor being 1.37).

iii. Those without a driving licence had greater odds than those with a driving licence to come into this category, the estimated factor being 1.16.

iv. Those with higher levels of recent job experience were less likely to be in this category, although the effect was small; each percentage increase in time in employment took about 0.002 off the odds.

With the exception of the age factor, which can probably be explained as before, these findings suggest that the 'submitted not placed' category reflects efforts by the Restart counsellors to help relatively disadvantaged people into placements. A young dependent child, a poor job record, and lack of a driving licence, are all potential barriers to employment for unemployed people. Furthermore, Restart office staff could be expected to have a reasonable degree of knowledge about all these background circumstances.

The fact that individuals with these characteristics tended to end in the 'submitted not placed' rather than the 'placed' category would, possibly, tend to reflect their continuing disadvantage in competing for a finite number of places.

'Referred (to DRO etc.)'. As in the case of the previous category, there was a positive influence from the individual's start-week of claim, although in this instance it was much smaller. Alternative interpretations can be applied, as before.

There were three other strong influences. One was whether or not the individual had a limiting disability or ill-health. This raised the odds of being 'referred' by a factor of about 1.6. Main channels of referral are to a Disablement Resettlement Officer, and possibly to a Claimant Adviser for guidance on application for invalidity status. This finding is, therefore, as expected.

There was, in addition, a marked influence of age. Those aged under 25 had much reduced odds of being 'referred' relative to any other age group. Those aged 55 or over had nearly 3.5 times the odds of under-25s of being referred.

Finally, those with a single child under five years old also had somewhat increased odds of being referred.

'Refused offer – not referred for review'. Referral, for review of the individual's entitlement to benefit, could take place as a result of refusal of an offer of placement. In this Restart group no referral takes place despite the initial refusal of offer.

The odds of refusal followed by no referral were much reduced in local labour markets where there was a relatively rapid turnover of unemployed claimants. Generally speaking, such local labour markets can be regarded as offering relatively good chances for unemployed people to get back to work. In these circumstances, it seems, refusal of an offer was less likely to be overlooked (see also the next group of findings below).

There were two further significant influences identified in this analysis:

i. An age effect once more, with over-45s having increased odds of refusing an offer (and not being referred) compared with under-25s.

ii. A qualification effect: those with technical or vocational qualifications having lower odds of refusing an offer (and not being referred).

The age effect could reflect both a greater tendency for older unemployed people to refuse placements, and an unwillingness of Restart staff to initiate a referral in these cases. The other influence was less straightforward to interpret. It seems that unemployed people are less likely to refuse an offer of placement, and then not be referred, if they are in circumstances which are favourable to chances of getting a job (such as a favourable local labour market, or a favourable qualification). Possibly individuals are more likely to refuse a placement in the first place if they feel they have good chances of getting a job; and Restart office staff may allow a refusal as reasonable for this same reason.

'Declined offer – referred for review'. This small group represents the situation where refusal of an offer does result in referral, presumably for checking entitlement to benefit.

The importance of local labour market circumstances to this kind of decision on the part of Restart office staff was confirmed by the analysis. Those in areas of high labour market turnover, and in inner city areas, were *more* likely to be referred after a refusal. (The former effect was a strong one, the latter on the borderline of statistical significance.) Taking up the interpretation proposed for the previous category, we would suggest that Restart office staff are more likely to regard a refusal of assistance as unreasonable when the local labour market environment is adverse and hence job prospects are relatively poor.

There were also two effects relating to personal characteristics:

i.   Women were more likely to be referred after a refusal of placement, than were men. This was a major difference, with women's odds of being referred under these circumstances being two and a half times those of men.

ii. Those lacking an educational qualification were more likely to be referred than those with such qualification. This difference, however, was of borderline significance.

The higher probability of women being referred might be linked with their responsibilities for children, if these clash with availability for placements. The analysis took account of marital status, number of children, and presence of children under five, but their effects (none of which was significant) were averaged over men and women. It seemed worthwhile, in this case, to re-estimate the analysis with separate family composition effects for men and women. This further analysis, however, did not indicate that there was a significant difference between men and women in these respects, so it seems that women's marital and family caring roles do not in themselves explain why they were more often referred for review.

'Offer not appropriate'. This category appeared to be related to only one of the variables in our analysis. Those with a disability or problem of ill-health had significantly reduced odds of being in this category. This may simply reflect a lower chance, for this group, of getting an opportunity outside the Restart process. (See also the section on the 'placed' category, above, where it was noted that those with disability or ill-health had equal chances of obtaining a placement.) On the other hand, a single significant relationship, in an analysis covering numerous factors, might arise purely by chance. Accordingly, not much weight should be placed upon this finding.

'Excused interview'. This substantial category had more distinguishing features than any other Restart group.

i.   Those located in areas of high labour market turnover had higher odds of being in this category, and those located in inner city areas had reduced odds.

ii. The earlier the unemployment claim had begun, the higher were the odds of being in this category.

iii. They aged 45 or over had reduced odds of being in this category, by comparison with younger workers.

iv. Women had higher odds than men of being in this category.

v.   Those with a child aged under five had reduced odds.

vi. Householders in local authority rented accommodation also had reduced odds.

vii. The higher the levels of recent job experience, the higher the odds of being in this category.

Taken as a whole, these attributes could be interpreted in terms of various forms of flexibility with respect to getting jobs. They accord with the fact that claimants were excused interview largely because they were moving into jobs or had good short-term prospects of doing so.

'Failed to attend interview'. This is the other category not reaching the Restart interview stage, but it is much less clearly connected with personal characteristics or labour market conditions

than the 'excused interview' group. Only two characteristics were associated with the category:

i. Age: those under 35 had much higher odds of being in this group, relative to those over 35. There was also a marked age trend, with older age groups having progressively lower odds of being classified as 'failed to attend'.

ii. Ethnic group: People of Afro-Caribbean descent had higher odds of being classified as 'failed to attend' relative to the 'white' ethnic group.

Summary of section. The analyses have provided a reasonably helpful view of the way the Restart 'actions' are applied to different types of client (although one must be aware that the picture will probably be very far from complete).

Earlier it was noted that the most positive impacts of Restart, in terms of people's personal reactions and perceptions, tended to be concentrated in the 'placed', 'submitted', and 'referred (to DRO, etc.)' categories. The present analyses add to our understanding of this, by showing that these 'actions' were distributed in a way which was broadly even-handed, and if anything favoured those with various disadvantages in the labour market. It is true that 'placement' itself was less available to women and to over-55s, which may have reflected characteristics of the ET programme. However, older workers, as well as those with disabilities or health problems, had higher access to 'referral', and those with a young child (known to be associated with reduced chances of employment) had positive chances both of being 'submitted' and of 'referral'. There was no indication that 'creaming' was taking place through Restart, since those with superior qualifications or superior recent job experience gained no systematic advantage in terms of the actions taken following Restart interviews.

The other main finding, from this group of analyses, concerns the extent to which the operation of Restart is affected by labour market conditions. This was most noticeable in regard to the Restart counseller's choice whether or not to make a referral for review of benefit claim after an offer had been refused. It seemed that (on average) favourable conditions in the local job market influenced the counsellor to overlook such refusals while unfavourable conditions influenced towards referral for review of benefit claim. Overall, overlooking refusal was more common than review, by a ratio of nearly six to one, but this may have reflected the generally buoyant labour market conditions of 1989, when the first stage of the interview took place. The operation of Restart may have been particularly sensitive in this respect to the worsening labour market conditions of 1990-91.

While we have spoken so far as if the Restart 'action' categories were entirely in the choice of the Restart counsellors, it should be recognised that the clients also influence what happens in Restart. Earlier on, for example, we saw that those saying they had responded positively to the Restart letter (e.g., in terms of job search) were more likely to be 'placed' or 'submitted'. This might have been the result of selective memory, but it might also be a case of personal effort influencing the Restart officer's actions.

The importance of 'self-selection' is most clearly seen with the two groups who do not reach a Restart interview. The larger of the two groups, those 'excused interview', was much the most distinctive category within Restart. Evidently, as they did not reach the Restart interview, no process of selection within Restart can apply to these. More generally, it is prudent to assume that processes of self-selection are operating within Restart alongside and in interaction with processes of allocation by the Restart counsellors.

Differences in Restart perceptions and contents

Earlier sections in this chapter have outlined how clients perceived Restart and what topics of substance were discussed in the Restart interviews. We now briefly review how these aspects varied between people in different circumstances or with different characteristics. Exactly the same method is applied as was used for the examination of Restart 'actions' in the previous section.[5]

Helpfulness of Restart interview. Rating of the Restart interview as helpful was associated with four personal characteristics of the respondent:

i.   Age: those over 35 had higher odds of experiencing the interview as helpful, than younger people.

ii. Ethnic group: those of Asian descent had the highest odds of experiencing the interview as helpful.

iii. Marital status: single people had higher odds of viewing the interview as helpful than did married people.

iv. Young children: those with one or more children under five had higher odds of experiencing the interview as helpful.

These findings add some further support to the view that Restart tended to operate somewhat in favour of groups with some labour market disadvantage.

Follow-up Restart interview. A wide range of circumstances or characteristics was associated with having a second Restart interview.

i. Where the local labour market was favourable (high local labour market turnover, or large reduction in unemployment level) there was an increased odds of taking part in a second interview.

ii. Men had higher odds of second interviews than women.

iii. Those who were separated or divorced had higher odds of receiving second interviews than either married or single people.

iv. Those with a young child had higher odds of taking part in a second interview than those without.

v. Those lacking a driving licence had higher odds of receiving a second interview than those having a driving licence.

vi. The lower the level of recent job experience, the higher the odds of having a follow-up interview.

While not all items here fit neatly together (and doubtless there are various reasons why second interviews take place), the general impression is again that Restart's resources were being directed more towards those likely to have difficulties in the labour market. On the other hand, follow-up interviews were more available in favourable local labour market conditions.

Five key topics. The main topics of Restart interviews, which might lead towards positive outcomes for clients, were jobs, referral to DRO or ERC, ET, EAS, and Job Clubs.

Discussing *jobs* with the Restart counsellor was independent of any of the personal characteristics in our usual list. But those in areas of high labour market turnover (probably meaning a favourable local job market) had increased odds of discussing jobs at their Restart interviews.

Referral to DRO or ERC depended, as one would expect, very largely on whether the individual had a disability or limiting problem of ill-health.

In contrast with the two previous items, discussion of ET was linked to quite a wide range of circumstances or characteristics. For reasons already noted, older workers (over 45) and women had much reduced odds of having a discussion of ET. On the other hand, people lacking any educational qualifications, lacking a driving licence, and having a relatively low level of recent job experience, all had increased odds of discussing ET. Finally, the odds of discussing ET were higher for those beginning their claim relatively late in the survey period – an indication either of changing labour market circumstances, over the four-month sampling period, or of changing policy and practice with respect to ET.

Discussions of *EAS* were, as in the case of ET, to have lower odds of occurrence both for women and for workers over 55. In other respects, however, there were marked differences between the groups discussing opportunities in the two programmes. Those aged 25-35, or 45-55, had higher odds of discussing EAS, compared with those in other age-bands. Those with educational qualifications and/or a driving licence also had increased odds of being involved in discussing this topic.

The discussion of *Restart courses* was to a large degree linked similarly to personal characteristics as in the case of ET discussions. Women, over-55s, those with educational qualifications, those with a driving licence, and those with relatively good recent job experience, all had reduced odds of discussing this topic in their Restart interviews. Two further personal characteristics increased the odds of discussing this possibility: being divorced or separated, or being of Afro-Caribbean descent. Labour market characteristics were also influential. Those in inner city areas had much lower odds of having Restart courses brought to their attention, while those with later start dates for their claims had higher odds.

The suggestion to consider joining a *Job Club* (made outside of Restart as well as in Restart) was made less often to women than to men. Like EAS, this was a topic which two age-groups had particularly high odds of considering in their Restart interviews: those aged 25-35, and those aged 45-55. Those without driving licences also had increased odds of being offered this suggestion. Job Clubs had reduced odds of being suggested in inner city areas and in areas of high labour market turnover.

Summary of section. These analyses, directed upon details of what happens within Restart, tend to support and develop the picture from the previous section referring to the broad Restart 'action' categories. But the analyses also bring to light some complications.

Restart appears to be particularly appreciated by those with some labour market disadvantages. There is also considerable evidence, from these further analyses, of discussions of placement possibilities being particularly directed towards groups with disadvantages.

From the viewpoint of a neat and tidy explanation, however, it is unfortunate that there is only a very partial correspondence between the groups finding Restart most helpful, and the groups apparently being given most help. It is true that the 25-35s and 45-55s seem to get special treatment in both EAS and Job Clubs, and these are among the appreciative groups. However, 35-45s are also appreciative but do not appear to get any special treatment. Those of Asian descent are appreciative, but do not get any extra access to Restart topics (do they, perhaps, enter the process with lower expectations?). This also applies to single people. Those with young children, the final appreciative group, get some slight additional access to Restart courses.

What these comparisons may point to is the possible importance, to some people at least, of qualitative aspects of the Restart interviews which are not captured by a simple list of topics discussed or opportunities offered. There is further information, within the survey interviews, on some of these qualitative aspects of the Restart interviews. We have not pursued the analysis in that direction, because it leads away from the central aims of the evaluation study. However, further analysis could be merited in the future.

As already indicated, this picture of the way opportunities are discussed with different groups is broadly reassuring from the viewpoint of non-discriminatory treatment, and indeed of positive assistance to individuals with disadvantages. There is however one exception. In these analyses, women emerge as having lower odds of receiving a number of types of suggestion, while not having better odds in respect of any type of suggestion. It should also be noted that these are the findings of analyses in which the average effects of qualifications, marital status and family composition have been statistically netted out. These analyses, however, do not explain why there should be such differences. The differences might arise (a) because of the way in which Restart interviews were being conducted; (b) because of differences in the content of the programmes (for instance, ET is known to have lower female participation and self-employment, relating to EAS, is also an area of generally low female participation); or (c) because a lower proportion of women have interests in the programmes which are available – a point closely related to (b). The data from the survey do not permit these possibilities to be distinguished in practice.

Restart 'actions' and further outcomes: initial analysis

This chapter has so far attempted to provide a picture of Restart in operation. In the final section, we wish to proceed to an initial insight into the nature of the analysis task for the evaluation study. The characteristics of Restart determine what can be done in the analysis (and what cannot be done). The best way of illustrating this is by means of some initial analyses at a relatively simple level, making use of comparisons between the Restart 'actions'.

As a first step, consider the proportions of the survey sample who were in employment at the time of the first survey interview, nearly six months after entry to the Restart process (and about one year from commencement of unemployment claim). For the survey as a whole, this proportion was 28 per cent.[6] For the Restart 'actions', the proportions were as shown in Table 3.7.

Table 3.7   Short-term employment outcome after Restart

Restart groups	% of each group employed at first survey interview
Placed	23
Submitted, not placed	25
Referred (to DRO, etc.)	18
Declined offer & referred	21
Declined offer - not referred	15
Offer not appropriate	35
Excused interview	51
Failed to attend	40

The employment level among the groups not interviewed for Restart, namely 'excused interview' and 'failed to attend', was considerably higher than for the remaining groups. The 'offer not appropriate' group also had a relatively high employment level, although not as high as for 'excused interview' or 'failed to attend'. This, of course, is in no sense an adverse reflection upon Restart. It reflects the selective mechanisms of the labour market. People were excused interview, in many cases, because they already had jobs. Presumably, others having jobs did not trouble to inform the local office and were classified as 'failed to attend'. Restart interviews took place with those left in unemployment after this process. These would have been expected to have lower chances of being in a job, at a later reference point, by comparison with those moving earlier into employment, for two reasons. First, they probably on average had less advantageous characteristics from the viewpoint of competing in the job market. Second, the chances of staying in a job, for someone who has one, are much better than the chances of moving into a job, for someone who is without one.

The differences in outcomes shown in Table 3.7 therefore do not reflect the relative effectiveness of different Restart actions, but processes of selection: different Restart actions apply to people with different characteristics or in different circumstances. Ideally, one would like to estimate the relationship between Restart action and outcome net of the characteristics or circumstances which affect selection into the Restart action. However, because this study did not focus upon the selection or decision process at the interview, we are far from being able to do so in a rigorous way.[7] Nevertheless, even a crude analysis, in which the more obvious factors involved in unemployment are controlled, is worth doing. So we carried out a relatively simple analysis[8] in which the variable to be explained or predicted was 'being employed at the first survey interview' and the explanatory variables consisted of (a) the usual set used in the multivariate analyses of this and of later chapters, together with (b) the Restart action group, expanded by the addition of 'unclassified' and 'control group' categories. To assess the effects of the Restart 'actions', the control group was taken as the reference group for this analysis: that is, its effect was set to zero and the effects of the other Restart groups measured relative to it.

The results of the analysis indicated significant influences from many of the characteristics or circumstances being modelled. The odds of being employed at the time of the first survey interview were raised by being in an area with high labour market turnover; by being female; by being young; by having a vocational qualification, and/or a driving licence; by being married; by not having a young child; by not being a householder tenant of council rented accommodation; and, above all, by having a good record of recent employment.

Even after statistically netting out these influences, there were significant differences among the Restart groups, which are summarised in Table 3.8. The effects shown in the table should be thought of as multiplying the odds of being employed, by comparison with the odds for members of the control group. An effect of less than one means that the group in question has relatively low or unfavourable odds of being employed, while an effect of more than one means that it has relatively high or favourable odds. The results have also been translated into probabilities of being in employment at

Table 3.8 Employment at first survey interview related to Restart Action Group

Restart action group	Relative odds of employment at first survey interview
Placed	n.s.
Submitted, not placed	n.s.
Referred (to DRO, etc.)	0.61
Declined offer & referred	n.s.
Declined offer - not referred	0.45
Offer not appropriate	1.55
Excused interview	2.81
Failed to attend	1.90
Unclassified	n.s.

Note: n.s. = not significantly different from 1.

Notes: (1) See text for other variables included in the analysis; (2) Estimates should be regarded only as first approximations as the model does not represent selectivity.

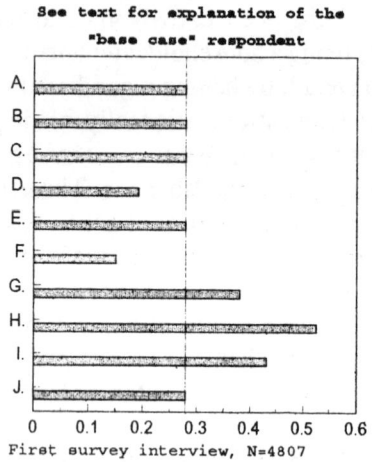

Fig. 3.1 Probability of being employed at the first survey interview, by Restart "action"

A. "Base case" respondent
B. "Placed"
C. "Submitted"
D. "Referred (to DRO etc.)"
E. "Refused offer - not referred"
F. "Refused offer - referred for review"
G. "Offer not appropriate"
H. "Excused interview"
I. "Failed to attend"
J. Outcome of Restart interview not known

Note: A bar touching the vertical line indicates "not significantly different from the base case"

See text for explanation of the "base case" respondent

First survey interview, N=4807

the time of the first survey interview, and presented in chart form in Figure 3.1 (see Chapter 1 for further details on graphical presentation of results).

These findings confirm that, even when the effects of many other characteristics have been netted out, the differences between the Restart groups persist much as they were shown in Table 3.7:

- The 'placed', 'submitted', and 'declined offer – not referred for review' groups had employment chances very similar to those for the control group.

- Those in the 'referred to DRO etc.' and 'declined offer – referred for review' groups had substantially lower employment chances than the control group.

- Finally, those in the 'offer not appropriate' group, and in the two groups not reaching a Restart interview, had considerably better employment chances than the control group.

What this analysis perhaps makes clearer than Table 3.7 is the diversity of outcomes across the Restart groups, a diversity which reflects not only differences between individuals or between circumstances, but also the selective processes in the labour market which interact with selective processes within Restart itself.

Any Restart effect is likely to be quite small by comparison with this background diversity. Nor can a Restart effect be associated with any one sub-group, whether defined in terms of a Restart action or otherwise. Restart is a process applied across the whole sample, although in different ways for different people; even those making an early exit get at least one Restart letter and may have other contacts with the Restart office (for example, to become excused from interview). It is the average impact of Restart across all these groups which creates a Restart effect, if any.

These considerations determine how the control group is to be used to assess the Restart effect. A comparison between the control group and any one or more Restart groups may tell one something about the latter groups (as in the analysis just discussed), but it tells one nothing about the overall Restart effect. The control group itself has to be thought of as a cross-section of all the characteristics and circumstances and selective processes which applies across Restart, with the single exception that the Restart process is absent. The Restart effect can only be measured by comparing the control group with *all* Restart groups in combination.

4   The Continuing Chance of Unemployment

In this chapter we begin our analysis of the effects of the Restart process, an analysis which continues over four chapters in all. The present chapter will give the most comprehensive view of those effects, because the outcome measure on which it focuses is that of *remaining unemployed or ceasing to be unemployed*.

Claimant unemployment

The definition of unemployment used in the design of this study, it should be recalled, is based on *claimant status* rather than (as in the ILO definition) on employment status and job search. At the time of sampling, all individuals by definition had unemployed claimant status. Subsequently they could leave that status in various ways, of which the following are the most important:

- They could get a job or become self-employed

- They could enter Employment Training (ET) or another programme such as a Restart Course

- They could go into full-time education

- They could give up their claim *without* having entered any of the situations listed above. This could reflect either that they no longer sought or were available for employment (as in the case of a woman having a baby, for instance), or that they no longer sought or had an entitlement to unemployment benefit (as in the case of someone transferring to sickness benefit, for instance).

For the purposes of this chapter's analysis, all these routes out of claimant unemployment are treated as one. We are only concerned with whether a claim to unemployed status persisted or did not persist, not with what was being done instead. The next two chapters will examine what happened 'on the other side' of unemployment, so to speak, and how Restart affected more specific outcomes such as getting a job or an ET placement.

The importance of the outcome
It has been more usual, in research on unemployment, to focus upon movements specifically into employment or self-employment, as the central outcome measure. There are several reasons, in the present study, for paying more attention to claimant or non-claimant status as an outcome.

a. The aims of Restart were not confined to employment. They encompassed movements into ET or other programmes when appropriate and review of entitlement to unemployment claim or alternative claimant status.

b. Accordingly, the only outcome measure capable of encompassing the aims and actions of Restart was continuation or termination of unemployed claimant status.

c. The effect upon claimant status, with its direct implications for Exchequer costs, is obviously relevant to a financial evaluation of Restart.

d. From a technical viewpoint, there is a particularly good chance of detecting a Restart effect through measures of claimant status, precisely because they can be expected to aggregate several smaller, component effects. (But this will only be true if the component effects all go in the same direction and do not cancel each other out.)

In stating that the claimant/non-claimant distinction offers the most comprehensive outcome measure for Restart, it is not being suggested that this makes the other outcome measures less important in their own right. Other outcome measures have to be taken into consideration for an overall evaluation. One of the incidental benefits of using the overall claimant/non-claimant measures, is that it later obliges one to look carefully at movements off the unemployment register, not only into jobs or training, but also into non-claimant status. This last is a type of transition from unemployment which has been greatly neglected in most research, including our own before now.

Descriptive measures

The design of the study (see Chapter 1) permits us to draw upon computerised administrative records to calculate claimant and non-claimant times. This can be done for the whole sample, including non-respondents, since the measures are independent of whether a survey interview took place. The period for which we had this information extended up to the end of June 1990, a little beyond the time when the last of the follow-up or second-wave survey interviews were held.

We used this administrative information to calculate measures of claimant time, beginning at a point six months after the start of the claim, and terminating at the end of June 1990. This represented an average of nearly 15 months from the start of the study period, excluding the five months or so leading up to the sampling point, with variation from 13 to 17 months, because the sample was built up continuously over a period of time.

Table 4.1 shows descriptive statistics for those passing through Restart and for the control group. As in all the analyses which we report (unless specifically stated to the contrary), the results have been re-weighted to correct for unequal sample fractions by Restart groups (see Chapter 1 for details).

Table 4.1 Claimant time after Restart date: whole sample

	Controls	Restart
Sample size (unweighted)	528	7661
a. For those who left the claimant register by June 1990: average days from start of claim to leave claimant register	*weighted data*	
	321	306
b. Proportions continuously on the claimant register to June 1990	21 %	14 %
c. Proportion of time on register, from Restart date to June 1990	58 %	54 %

This table first of all provides some useful background for interpreting Restart effects, and other influences upon unemployment. It must be remembered that the sample originally consisted of people approaching their sixth month of unemployment, in the current claim.

The table shows that, for such a group, a little more than half the time over the next 15 or so months was spent in unemployment (item (c) in the table). This can be compared with an average of 35 per cent of time in unemployment, during the period 1982-87 inclusive (or whatever part of it was relevant to the individual), for the same sample. Currently, therefore, this group was spending more of its time in unemployment than previously, even though the labour market through much of 1989 was a reasonably favourable one. This raised level of unemployment for the sample can simply be explained by the fact that the sample had been selected on the basis of already having spent nearly six months in their current claim. They were therefore implicitly selected as a group having current difficulties in the job market.

The table also shows that at the end of the study period, about 15 per cent had *never* left unemployment throughout the period (item (b) in the table). This also implies that 85 per cent had left unemployment *at some time*, but not necessarily permanently.

Further, the table shows that, on average, it took the members of this sample about 10 months to leave the register (or four months from Restart), provided that one *excludes* those on the register throughout the period (item (a) in the table). If we could take account of the actual exit-times of those on the register throughout the period, then naturally the overall average would be increased. This will be addressed later in the chapter through the statistical technique survival analysis.

Initial indication of Restart effect. The chief interest of Table 4.1 is that it suggests the existence of a Restart effect which tends to reduce the time spent in an unemployed claimant status. Each of the three descriptive indicators (a-c in the table) points in the same direction.

- Item (c) shows a difference, in the average proportion of time on the register, of about four per cent over the period, with the control group spending more time on the register.

- Item (a) shows the control group members taking, on average, five per cent longer to leave the claimant register, if they had done so by June 1990.

• Item (b) provides the strongest indication of a Restart effect, showing that 21 per cent of the control group were still on the register at June 1990 (and had never left it), while this applied to 14 per cent of the Restart group.

It must be appreciated that these figures come from a sample and, because they are subject to sampling error, their reliability must be statistically tested, as we shall do in the course of more elaborate analyses shortly.

A similar analysis can be carried out for those who had a first survey interview, and for those who also had a second survey interview. In this case, however, we can use the recollections of the survey respondents to cross-check with the administrative records. (Later, when we wish to look at the proportions of time spent in jobs, on ET, or in economic inactivity, respondents' recall will be the sole source of information.) In Table 4.2, a single indicator from this source (equivalent to item (c) in Table 4.1) is shown.

Table 4.2   Proportion of time unemployed

weighted data

	First survey interview		Second survey interview	
	Control	Restart	Control	Restart
Sample size (unweighted)	240	4567	186	3233
Proportion of time on register, from Restart date (weighted)	73 %	66 %	59 %	54%

Note: weighting corrects for unequal sampling fractions by Restart action group.

The result at the second interview was very close to the result obtained using the administrative data to June 1990. This increases confidence in the reliability of the interview information. The other points of interest from the table concern the picture at the time of the first interview, about six months after the Restart date. As would be expected, the proportion of time spent as unemployment claimants was considerably greater up to the first interview than over the whole survey period. Further, the analysis shows a rather greater Restart effect, of about seven per cent by comparison with the control group, at the time of the first interview.

Interpreting the Restart effect. There are several reasons for expecting that the results shown in Table 4.1 will be reliable. They are based on large, nationally representative samples which are free of sample clustering effects. They are completely unaffected by non-response to the survey. And they come from comparisons between those entering the Restart process and a randomly allocated control group (tests of bias in the control group have been discussed in Chapter 1).

So, although we will shortly present the findings from much more elaborate analyses, using multivariate techniques, it should not be thought that the simple results of Table 4.1 are in some sense defective. On the contrary, our later analyses will show that they are robust. Multivariate analysis will, however, permit us to do some things which a simple descriptive approach cannot do, such as coming to an overall assessment which combines items (a) and (b) of Table 4.1. It will also provide the general reassurance which comes of looking at things from various points of view.

Some initial impression of how Restart makes a difference can perhaps be obtained by tabulating the same descriptive statistics for the various 'Restart actions' recorded by the Restart staff (see Chapter 3 for details). Since this information was also available for the whole sample, not just for those who had a survey interview, we can do this unaffected by non-response effects.

At the end of Chapter 3, it was stressed that the effects of Restart could not be identified with any particular Restart actions or aspects without great care in interpretation. Because Restart actions are likely to be selectively applied, and to reflect the personal inclinations or characteristics of clients, the groups concerned are not directly comparable. If we are careful not to interpret the table in this invalid way, we can nonetheless pick out some useful hints about features of the different groups.

One obvious comparison is between members of the 'placed' group and those in the 'submitted, not placed' group. Members of both groups have been selected for placement by Restart counsellors, but for the 'submitted' group no placement has been achieved. Table 4.3 confirms that those placed had less subsequent claiming than those

Table 4.3   Claiming indicators for Restart 'action' categories

	% of time claiming 1988-90	mean time (days) to leave register	% still on register at June 1990
'Placed'	54	304	10
'Submitted'	61	336	19
'Referred'	61	353	20
'Refused offer, not referred'	66	358	26
'Refused offer, referred'	51	319	10
'Offer not appropriate'	54	304	16
'Excused interview'	29	215	2
'Failed to attend'	46	262	9

Base: total sample (N=8189). Source: JUVOS data.

submitted but not placed through Restart. But one has to keep in mind, as was described in Chapter 3, that the 'submitted not placed' group had several characteristics which would tend to be disadvantageous in the labour market.

Another natural comparison is between the two groups who declined an offer of being submitted to a placement, one of which was then referred for review of entitlement to benefit claim, while the other was not. Those in the group not referred for review of claim were much less likely to remain on the register. On the face of it, this might be taken as evidence to support a policy of more frequent referral of claim. But it might rather illustrate the complexities involved in comparisons between groups when there are selection and choice processes determining those groups. The lower average level of claiming of the group referred for review of claim was (as will be shown in a later analysis) chiefly the result of withdrawal into economic inactivity, while the group not referred for review of claim subsequently maintained a level of attachment to the labour market which was in line with that of the whole sample. The Restart counsellor may well, and presumably should, make a judgement about whether or not the individual's rejection of an offer of placement indicates a general lack of interest in employment.

The final points in Table 4.3 to which we draw attention concern the 'excused interview' group. This group spent far less of the study period as claimants than did the other Restart categories. This is as would be expected, since the basis for being excused the Restart interview was that the individual was leaving the register in one way or another. But it was clearly not the case that most of the people in this had actually left the register by the time when the Restart interview would fall due. In fact, only half had done so. Being placed in this category, then, was often not a rubber-stamping of change of status which had already taken place, but involved judgement by the local staff about the probability of changes ahead. Sometimes, expected moves off the register did not take place. This evidence also suggests that many if not all of the 'excused interview' category would have been on the register sufficiently long for one or more contacts to take place with the local office concerning Restart, even though a Restart interview did not take place

Multivariate analyses of claimant time

We have already made it clear that, when we turn to multivariate analyses, it is not because the descriptive statistics are unreliable. Nevertheless, multivariate analyses will permit us to advance the evaluation in several respects.

1. They permit us simultaneously to test the significance of the Restart effect and to compare its size and significance with the effects of other important influences upon unemployment outcomes.

2. They permit us to see whether the Restart effect is robust across several different methods of analysis.

3. They make it possible to examine composite measures of effect.

4. They open the way to assessing some interesting though subsidiary issues, notably the effect of non-response to the survey.

Undoubtedly the first of these reasons for pursuing multivariate methods has much the most practical importance. If we show that the effect of Restart is (say) a five per cent reduction in time claiming, is that to be interpreted as low or high, small or large? One of the best ways of getting a feel for the answer is to see how the Restart effect compares with other effects, when they appear side by side in a joint analysis.

Change in claimant time

Tables 4.1-4.3 have considered the percentage of time spent as an unemployment claimant in the period after Restart. In some respects, however, it is better to use a more complex measure, which reflects the *difference or change* in time spent as an unemployed claimant, between the period before the claim and the period after Restart. We can then assess how far Restart results in a *relative reduction* in time spent claiming.

There are two main advantages in this approach. One is that it results in a measure which has a more nearly normal distribution, which widens the scope for multivariate analysis and simplifies interpretation. The second reason is that by using a change measure, we can expect to reduce the effect of unmeasured influences which apply at both the earlier and the later periods. This is a particularly important consideration for analyses in which non-respondents are included, because then we have only a relatively small amount of explanatory information to deploy. For example, we do not have details of qualification for the non-respondents, but we can reasonably assume that the presence or absence of qualifications affected both the chances of being unemployed earlier on, and the chances of being unemployed more recently: the effects therefore tend to 'cancel out' if a change measure between the two periods is used.

Analysis with the whole sample. An analysis of the whole sample (including non-respondents to the survey) made use of the following items of information to attempt to explain change in the proportion of time spent claiming (for further details of the items, see Chapter 1).

- Change in local labour market unemployment, 1988-90 (change in the stock)

- Ratio of unemployment inflow and outflow to unemployment level, 1989 (a measure of the flow relative to the stock)

- Inner city area, or not

- The start week of the individual's claim (which controls for changes in the overall state of labour markets, over the time of the survey)

- Male or female
- Age (divided into five groups, so that non-linear relationships to age could be detected)
- Whether respondent or non-respondent to the survey
- Whether control group member or took part in Restart
- Proportion of time as unemployed claimant during 1982-1987

The analysis using the change measure, and with the influences of the other variables simultaneously estimated, confirmed the reliability of the difference suggested in Table 4.1, row (a). The sample members as a whole spent a higher proportion of time claiming, in 1989-90, than they had done in 1982-87, but the increase was less for those going through Restart than for control group members. The Restart effect estimated by this method was found to be, statistically speaking, highly significant.[1]

It is worth noting that most of the other types of influences included in the analysis proved to have significant effects upon change in unemployment claiming. The largest effects were those for females, where claiming rose relative to men, and for older people in the sample (45-54 and, still more, 55 or over), whose claiming rose relative to under-25s.

The analysis also showed that there were marked differences in outcomes between respondents and non-respondents, with the non-respondents reducing their claiming relative to respondents. Care has to be taken in interpreting this finding, since non-response in itself is obviously not a factor in unemployment; its apparent influence must result from one or more variables which are correlated both to non-response and to unemployment, not controlled in this analysis. A reasonable surmise is that non-response is linked to mobility, and that mobility is linked to a higher likelihood of leaving unemployment.

In these analyses, inclusion or exclusion of the non-response variable in the analysis had little effect on the estimation of the Restart effect. But the results showed that non-response was a sufficiently important influence to deserve further investigation through more elaborate statistical procedures, and we return to this following the next section of results.

Analysis based on those at the first survey interview. The chief limitation of the last analysis was that not many variables could be included, since we could only use those which were available for non-respondents as well as respondents. By turning to the survey interview data, a far wider range of variables can be brought into the analysis. This leads to a better assessment of the importance of the Restart effect, as well as providing interesting information about other influences upon claiming.

The same outcome measure was therefore analysed with data from the 4,807 respondents at the first interview. This analysis confirmed that there was a significant Restart effect: those passing through Restart had on average spent less time as claimants, up to June 1990, relative to their earlier claiming experience, than was the case for the control group.[2]

The statistical model from which these results came contained 24 terms or parameters, representing labour market effects, gender, age, qualifications, ethnic group, marital status, number of children, number of children aged under 5, limiting disability or ill-health, tenure (local authority rented housing), and whether or not a member of the control group. (For further details of these measures, as well as of various other measures which were considered but then discarded through a process of exploratory analysis, see Chapter 1).

Figure 4.1 portrays the results of the analysis in the form of a bar chart. The vertical line in the centre of the chart indicates the 'base case', that is, where a person with specified characteristics commonly encountered in the sample comes on the measure of change in proportion of time spent claiming. The various bars show how much each variable either increases or decreases an individual's claiming, around this base case (see Chapter 1 for further details). A number of terms in the model had effects which were not significantly different from zero, and these have been omitted from the figure. All those included in the diagram, conversely, were statistically significant. The reference values of the variables are set to zero, and so result in no deviation from the overall mean. In the case of age, for example, the reference or comparator group consisted of those aged less than 25. Looking at the figure, one can see that those aged 25 to 34 come below the centre line, and therefore have a greater fall in claiming relative to the under-25s, while all the other age groups are above the centre line, and therefore have a smaller fall in claiming than the under-25s.

The diagram suggests that, within the ranges of the variables considered in the diagram, only two were much greater in their effect than was Restart. Age was clearly the most powerful influence. The

**Fig. 4.1   Change in percentage of time claiming,
post-Restart compared with baseline period**

A. "Base case" respondent
B. Areas with highest
labour turnover
C. Areas with lowest
D. Areas with greatest
decline in unemployment
E. Areas with least
F. Latest start of claim
G. Earliest start
H. Female
I. Aged 25-34
J. Aged 45-54
K. Aged 55 plus
L. Indian or Pakistani
origin
M. 1 child under 5
N. Has driving licence
O. Renting from council
P. Control group member

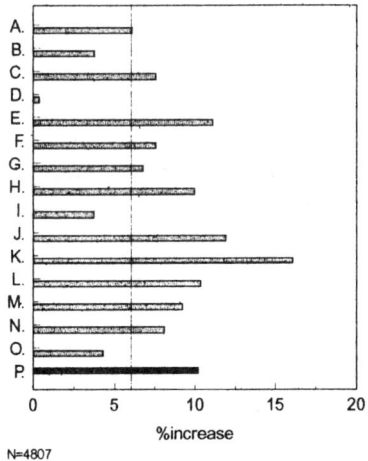

N=4807

local labour market was also important, with areas that had the greatest decline in unemployment also having much lower levels of claiming (relative to prior claiming histories) than those with the smallest decline in unemployment (recall that the period 1988-90 was one of universal reduction in unemployment levels). The Restart effect was of a very similar order to that of gender, ethnic origin, or having a young child.

One further point may be worth noting in passing. Educational and vocational qualifications were not significantly related to change in the proportion of time spent as a claimant, even though in previous research they have been among the most widely reported influences upon employment chances. There are two plausible interpretations for the lack of a qualification effect in the present case. One is that we are using change over time as the measure of outcome, and the effect of qualifications may be highly constant over time. The alternative is that qualifications has different relations with movement into employment and movement into a non-employed, non-claimant status, so that these cancel out when the outcome measure is claiming (which encompasses both).

Non-response treated as a selection effect

Non-response has already been shown as having a strong relationship to time spent in unemployment. For the total sample, it could be shown that the effect of Restart persisted even when differences between respondents and non-respondents were controlled. When we come to the more detailed analyses using data from the first survey interview, non-respondents are, of course, excluded. They have, in a sense, selected themselves out. But statistical techniques, developed in the last decade, permit us to take some account of the selected-out group, provided that we have information to distinguish them from the group which is selected-in. The technique is often referred to as 'sample selection modelling'.[3] In essence, the technique is first to estimate a model of the selection variable, and then to pass information from this first stage to the main analysis so as to make allowance for the selected-out part of the sample.

Because we should do everything possible to assure the reliability of our evaluation of the Restart effect, we decided that it would be worthwhile to make use of this approach. Before presenting our findings, however, we have to record some reservations. Sample selection modelling has rightly been called a 'fragile' technique.[4] Its effectiveness depends critically upon (a) having an adequate model of the selection variable – in this case, of what makes the difference between response and non-response; and (b) satisfying the stringent statistical assumptions for the analysis. In the present case, our information to explain non-response is certainly far from adequate. In fact, our model to explain non-response consists only of labour market variables, gender, and age, and this is incomplete. In particular, we believe that non-response reflects mobility, but at the time of the analysis we had no data on this subject. Possibly, also, non-response reflects social characteristics of neighbourhoods, on which we again lack information.

The analysis indicated that the sample selection effects were not of any great importance.[5] The revised estimates, with allowance for selection, in our main model were extremely close to those originally obtained, not only for the Restart variable, but for all other variables. The only real change resulting from the sample selection modelling procedure was to increase the error estimates and so reduce the significance levels. The estimated Restart effect remained significant.[6] In conclusion, there was little reason to suppose that non-response made a difference to our conclusions about the Restart effect (or other effects). (See Figure 4.2 for a graphical summary, similar in form to Figure 4.1.)

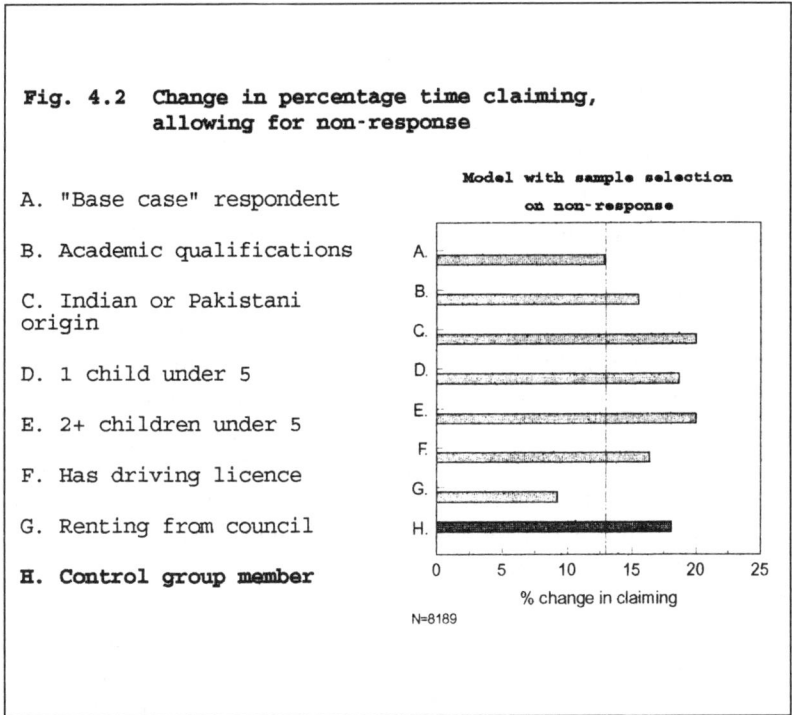

Fig. 4.2 Change in percentage time claiming, allowing for non-response

A. "Base case" respondent

B. Academic qualifications

C. Indian or Pakistani origin

D. 1 child under 5

E. 2+ children under 5

F. Has driving licence

G. Renting from council

H. Control group member

N=8189

Elapsed time to the end of the claim

So far we have considered claiming or non-claiming as a proportion of a set period of time. There are also other ways of assessing claiming over time. One, which has been widely adopted by social scientists in recent years, deals with the time taken to change from one status to another, and is often referred to as survival analysis. It may be helpful to summarise some of its main features from the specific point of view of the present analysis.

Given that our sample was by definition registered as unemployed at the time of sampling, an obvious question is how long it takes for the claim to come to an end, and whether or not that time is shorter for Restart participants than for the control group. It seems rather plausible that a procedure such as Restart, with a definite 'time discipline', might influence the timing of various events which bear upon the ending of unemployment.

Another important issue concerns those who remain as unemployed claimants for the whole of the survey period, and are still in that status at the end. How are these to be brought into the assessment? In fact, survival analysis allows for incomplete spells, by fitting them into a distribution of exit times estimated from the available data, and so assessing their likely termination times. In this important respect, therefore, survival analysis permits us to go beyond the time frame of the survey.

The other preliminary point to be made is simply that the information provided by an analysis of exit-times is very different from that provided by the earlier analysis of average proportions of times in a given status. This can be shown by an example. Suppose that we have two individuals, whom we call Alice and Zenia. Alice is unemployed for one month, then gets a job for six months, and is then unemployed for a further five months. Zenia is unemployed for six months, then employed for six months. Both Alice and Zenia have spent 50 per cent of the period as claimants, but Alice's exit-time from the initial claim was five months less than that of Zenia.

The previous example, as well as illustrating a simple point, gives some hint of the further complexities of analysing events over time. We do not pursue these complexities in this report. Our approach, outlined in Chapter 1, has been to apply the simplest statistical model to a relatively simple problem: that of estimating the exit-time from the initial claim only (while ignoring recurrent events, e.g. renewed claims, entirely).

Nevertheless, the results obtained within our limited approach lend strong support to the existence of a Restart effect. Furthermore, we did to some extent test the reliability of our simple approach, by varying the underlying distribution assumptions for our analyses (Chapter 1 provides further details for those interested). We found very similar results with each distribution assumption, which suggested that the analysis was robust.

As with the previous measure, we began by considering the whole sample, with the limited set of variables available for non-respondents as well as for respondents. Non-response itself was included as one of these variables. All the variables included in this analysis proved to be highly significantly related to exit-times from the initial claimant status. This was also true of the Restart effect, with the estimated time of leaving the claim being considerably greater for control group members. It is notable, in fact, that the significance of the Restart effect here was considerably greater than with the earlier analysis of changes in proportions of time spent claiming.[7]

The strengths of this analysis are the large sample size, the inclusion of non-respondents, and the use of a set of variables which, though limited, was of high quality. By using the additional information collected in the survey interviews, we were able to carry out confirmatory analyses which also permitted comparisons of the Restart effect with the effects of a wider range of variables.

The analysis with the usual set of explanatory variables from the survey was performed with the data from the first survey interview. The results were among the clearest obtained in this survey. They are summarised graphically in Figure 4.3, which shows the estimated average 'exit time' from unemployment for the 'base case' individual in the survey (the top bar in the chart) and for people differing from this reference person in specific ways.

The Restart effect was, once more, statistically highly significant.[8] It was also of a similar order of magnitude to the effects of most of the other significant variables, being clearly exceeded only by age and marital status.

In quantitative terms, a person in the control group was estimated to spend (on average) some 55 days more before first leaving claimant status than a person in Restart. This figure should not be taken too literally, as these types of quantitative estimates are sensitive to the statistical assumptions made in the analysis and to the omission of relevant variables. The reason why this figure is so much higher than the 15 days shown earlier in Table 4.1, is because the present estimate takes account of those still left on the register at the end of the study period, who are likely to spend particularly long periods in unemployment, while the earlier figure does not.

It is interesting to note, in passing, that the usual significant effect of educational qualifications, missing from the analysis of proportions of time claiming, was restored in the present analysis.

Fig. 4.3 Estimated time to leave unemployment

A. "Base case" respondent
B. Areas with highest labour turnover
C. Areas with lowest
D. Areas with greatest decline in unemployment
E. Areas with least
F. Inner city resident
G. Earliest start of claim
H. Latest start
I. Female
J. Aged 25-34
K. Aged 35-44
L. Aged 45-54
M. Aged 55 plus
N. Academic qualifications
O. Divorced/widowed
P. Single
Q. Has driving licence
R. Renting from council
S. Control group member
T. 100% claiming in 82-87
U. 0% claiming in 82-87

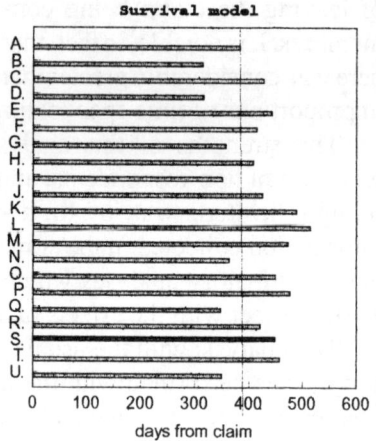

Survival model

(bar chart of days from claim for categories A–U; x-axis: 0, 100, 200, 300, 400, 500, 600; labelled "days from claim")

N=4807

Is there an 'early exit' effect of Restart?

It might be assumed that the effect of Restart depends upon passing through the Restart interview. It is also possible, however, that part at least of the effect is anticipatory. The arrival of a letter asking the person to come to a Restart interview could in itself stimulate action or alter the timing of actions that were already being planned. In view of the particularly clear evidence of a Restart effect upon the average time to exit from the initial claim, it is important to examine this surmise directly.

The practical problem in doing so is to decide what constitutes an early exit from Restart – early enough, that is, to be the result of an anticipatory action on the part of the individual concerned, rather than a result of passing through the Restart interview. We decided to base the cut-off on the median exit times for the group classified as 'excused interview'. Reasons for individuals to be excused in this way were usually that they had got a job or placement, or were shortly expecting to move into one, or had left the register for some other reason. By definition, therefore, they consisted of 'early exits'. Although, in some cases, the expected moves off the register did not take place, so that the claim continued for a long period, use of the median duration is insensitive to these larger values, and represents the *typical* 'early exit'. The value was in fact 206 days, or about six months and three weeks. This is within a week or so of the typical Restart interview date. Applying this criterion identified just over 10 per cent of the sample as 'early exits'.

On this basis, all individuals interviewed at the first stage of the survey were classified as either 'early exits' or 'not early'. The usual set of variables was used to attempt to explain this difference.[9] In this analysis, the Restart effect was found to be not significantly different from zero, so that the notion of a specifically 'early' Restart effect was not supported.

It is of interest to note the circumstances or characteristics which were statistically related to early exits from the unemployed register. These were:

- being in an area with high labour market turnover
- being young (under-25); and especially, not being over 45
- being of Afro-Caribbean descent
- being married
- not having children under five
- not being a householder tenant in local authority rented accommodation.

These are, not surprisingly, very much the same list of factors which distinguished the 'excused interview' group from other Restart groups (as shown in Chapter 3). The significant effects are summarised graphically in Figure 4.4. The outcome measure has been converted, for ease of interpretation, into probabilities of being off the unemployed register at the time in question.

According to this analysis, there was no difference between men and women in terms of leaving the register at an early point. But some of the evidence which will be presented in Chapter 6 suggests that there is a greater tendency for women to move off the register into a non-claimant, non-employed status. Since such moves might be particularly influenced by the commencement of the Restart process, it seemed worthwhile to re-run the analysis, for women separately.[10]

Fig. 4.4 Probability of leaving unemployment "early"

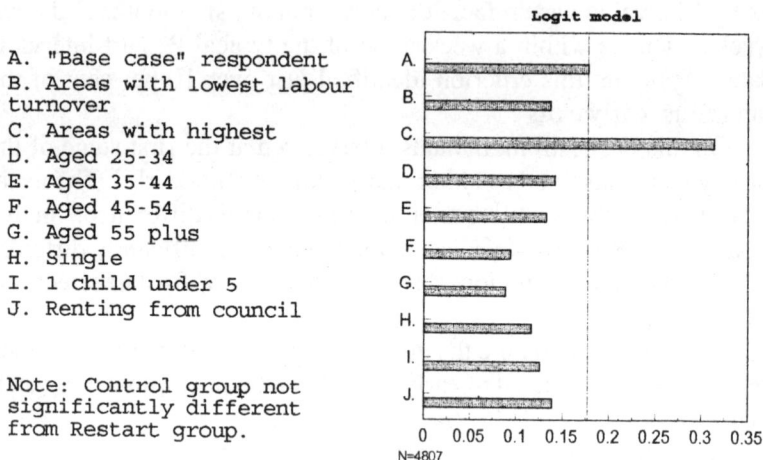

Logit model

A. "Base case" respondent
B. Areas with lowest labour turnover
C. Areas with highest
D. Aged 25-34
E. Aged 35-44
F. Aged 45-54
G. Aged 55 plus
H. Single
I. 1 child under 5
J. Renting from council

Note: Control group not significantly different from Restart group.

N=4807

In this case, the Restart effect could be deemed as just significant.[11] There was, therefore, support for the notion of Restart stimulating 'early exits' *in the case of women only*. The significant effects are summarised graphically in Figure 4.5, which is similar to Figure 4.4.

It is interesting to examine which other factors significantly influenced early exits from the register among women. The women more likely to leave the register early were those who:

• were married

• without children under five

• aged under 25 rather than 25-34

• living in areas with high labour market turnover

• and with relatively high levels of recent job experience.

These factors seem much more related to competition for jobs than to movement into a non-claimant, non-employed status.

Fig. 4.5 Women's probability of leaving
unemployment "early"

A. "Base case" respondent

B. Areas with lowest labour
turnover
C. Areas with highest

D. Aged 25-34

E. Divorced/widowed
F. Single

G. 0% employed in 1985-87
H. 100% employed

I. Control group member

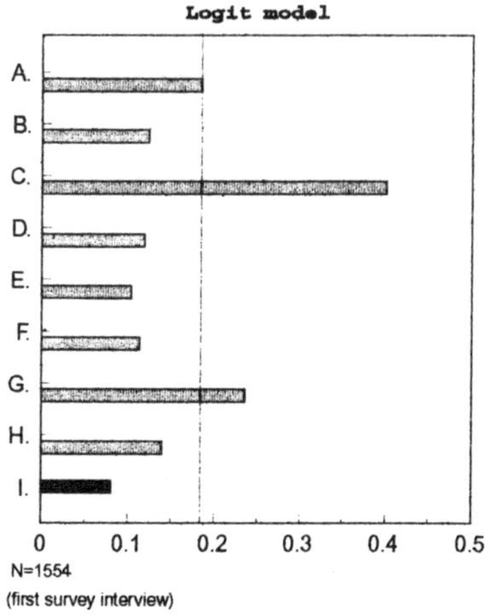

Logit model

N=1554
(first survey interview)

On the whole, the evidence of a specifically 'early' Restart effect must be regarded as rather weak. There was no overall significant effect, and the effect for women considered separately was only just significant. These results also have to be placed against the background of the survival analysis of exit times from unemployment, which indicated that there was a substantial Restart effect. If much of this effect had been concentrated in the early period, around the time of the Restart interview or before, then one would have expected to find a strong 'early exit' effect. The rather weak early effect found can easily be accommodated as merely a minor part of a more general Restart effect in accelerating exits from unemployment across the whole period of the study.

It remains possible, of course, that Restart may have had a greater effect on early exits from the register in the initial years of its development (1986-88). One might suppose that there was some 'shake-out' process over this period as a systematic procedure for checking the validity of claims was made universal. If this happened, it would seem that the effect had become a small one by the time of the present study.

Clarifying the time course of the Restart effect

The relatively weak and inconclusive results of the preceding section led us to try a different approach. We reverted to use of the whole sample, so as to be able to control for differences between respondents and non-respondents. Non-response might be particularly related to 'early exits', since the longer ago that unemployment ended, the less relevant the survey may have seemed to those approached. Reverting to the overall sample necessitated a simpler analysis, in the sense of having fewer explanatory variables. However, the Restart effect assessed through the control group seems not to be much affected by how many other variables are included. The approach in these further analyses was to divide the exits from the claimant register by applying several different 'cut-off points': so as well as looking at 'early exits', we looked at 'very early exits' and on 'not so early exits'.[12]

The 'very early' group was defined as leaving the register by six months (less than 183 days), and there were 4.1 per cent of the sample meeting this criterion. The 'early exit' group was defined just as before, with a criterion of less than 206 days to leave the register, and comprised 12.5 per cent of the sample when non-respondents were included. The 'not so early' group was selected a month further, and needed to leave the register in less than 236 days; that is, about seven and a half months, or about one month after the time of the Restart counselling interview. This last group incorporated 27.3 per cent of the total sample. The chief results of these analyses are shown in Table 4.4.

Consistent with the analysis of the preceding section, there was no significant effect at the 'early exit' stage, the middle row in the table above. The 'very early' condition, corresponding to a pre-Restart-interview stage, also showed no significant effect. But one month further on from the Restart interview, a powerful Restart effect was visible. As the table shows, the control group's odds of leaving the register by this time were only 0.67 (two-thirds) those of the Restart group's. The results for this post-Restart stage are summarised in chart form in Figure 4.6, with each significant effect being compared with the 'base case' individual in a similar way to previously. In this instance, however, the outcome measure has been converted, for

Table 4.4   Summary of Restart effects on claiming at various times

Timing	Estimate of Restart effect (relative odds of leaving register, for control group)	Significance tests (t-value)
Very early exit	1.05	n.s.
Early exit	1.07	n.s.
Not so early exit	0.67	-3.33

Note: n.s. means not significantly different from unity.

convenience of interpretation, into probabilities of being off the unemployed register at the cut-off point about one month after the Restart interview.

The models were also re-estimated allowing the Restart effect to take different values for the male and female sub-samples. However, this gender interaction never approached significance. So, the Restart effect seemed non-existent, for both men and women, at both the 'very early' and the 'early' exit points, but was equally significant for both men and women at the later exit point.

Why did a Restart effect fail to materialise for women at the 'early' stage, contrary to the findings of the previous section? A possible reason is the introduction of the non-response variable, which as expected was very strongly related to exit from the register at all the cut-off points. However, a conclusive explanation of the discrepancy concerning an early exit Restart effect for women, and concerning the interpretation of the non-response effect, will have to await further research.

These analyses seem to establish that, even if there is a small (for women alone) Restart effect quite early, *the main Restart effect appears in the month after the counselling interview*. In demonstrating this, we have also further verified the reality of the Restart effect, and the importance of the counselling interview and linked events in the month which follow it.

Fig. 4.6 Probability of leaving unemployment one month after Restart interview

A. Base case (non-Restart)
B. Areas with lowest labour turnover
C. Areas with highest labour turnover
D. Areas with lowest decline in unemployment
E. Areas with highest decline in unemployment
F. Inner city resident
G. Aged 25-34
H. Aged 35-44
I. Aged 45-54
J. Aged 55 plus
K. Female
L. Non-response
M. Restart participant

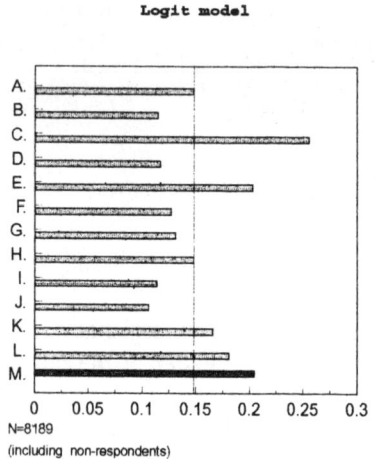

Logit model

N=8189
(including non-respondents)

Different Restart effects for different groups?

In the preceding section, we made use of statistical models which permitted the estimated Restart effect to take different values for men and for women. This is a good way of testing whether, in fact, there is a statistically reliable difference in the Restart effect by gender. The simple answer, as we have seen, is that there was no such gender difference.

The same approach can be applied, by repeated testing with different groups, to provide an answer to a question of considerable importance for policy: namely, was Restart tending to produce different results for different groups of clients? We have applied it, as well as to male-female differences, only to the case of age differences. Using the 'not so early' time criterion above, we divided the sample into three age groups (under-25, 25-44, 45-plus), and allowed the Restart effect to take different values for each age group. As in the case of the analysis by gender, we found no evidence to support the surmise that the Restart effect was different for different age groups.

In principle, this approach could have been applied to many further analyses, both within this chapter and in following chapters. We have not done so, partly because of limitation upon resources for the analysis, and partly through a judgement that we would have been unlikely to find significant results. The differences between men and women, and between different age groups, were (if one took a view across all the analyses) much the most important in relation to the outcomes. Accordingly, these groups provided the greatest scope for different Restart effects to emerge. Further, when we turn to the more detailed analyses taken from the survey interviews, we have a reduced size of control group, and it becomes problematical to split it further into combinations with other variables. The analysis with the full survey sample, providing a control group of 528, makes the estimation of separate Restart effects a more feasible proposition. The fact that we found no significantly different Restart effects either by gender or by age, in these large-scale analyses, makes it unlikely, in our judgement, that such different Restart effects could be identified elsewhere. But this is not the same as to say that they do not exist.

Summary of chapter
This chapter has focused upon the broadest available measures of outcomes for the sample, namely those to do with being, or not being, an unemployed claimant. Non-claimant status incorporates jobs, participation in programmes such as ET or in full-time education, and economic inactivity.

The sample on average spent more than half of the 15 or so months of the study period on the unemployment register. About one in seven of them spent the whole period unemployed.

Simple indicators showed that those in the control group, when compared with those passing through Restart, spent a greater proportion of time unemployed, took longer on average to leave unemployment, and were more likely to be continuously unemployed throughout the study period.

Analyses using first the whole sample (including non-respondents), and then that part of the sample interviewed in the survey, confirmed that an effect of Restart persisted when the influences of numerous other variables were taken into account. For these analyses, we made use of a change measure, relating current unemployment to each individual's prior history of unemployment.

Non-respondents to the survey were found to spend less time in unemployment than respondents. The Restart effect persisted when the effect of non-response was taken account of in various ways.

Survival analysis was then used to estimate the 'exit times' from the initial unemployment, and to take account in doing so of those remaining with uncompleted spells of unemployment at the end. This analysis provided particularly strong evidence of a Restart effect.

A special analysis was conducted to examine the possibility that much of the Restart effect took place early on. Such an 'early exit' effect was found in the case of women only, and was just-significant. There was, therefore, only weak support for the notion of a specifically 'early' Restart effect.

As a development of this approach, movement off the register was examined (for the whole sample, including non-respondents) at three points: before, at the time of, and about a month after, the Restart interview. These analyses showed that a strong Restart effect had developed by about one month after the Restart interview. This provides further evidence of the reality of the Restart effect and probably confirms an important effect for the counselling interview and the immediately following actions.

Finally, tests were carried out to assess whether the Restart effect differed for men and for women, and between different age groups. The answer was that it did not, although it should be noted that the scope for such tests was limited by the size of the control group. In view of the fact that gender and age were the most important sources of differences in outcomes in this survey as a whole, it seems unlikely that the Restart effect would be found to vary if similar analyses were conducted with other groups.

5 Jobs and Training

When people cease to be claimants, what precisely do they do? And if Restart moves people out of unemployment, as the previous chapter indicated, what does it move them into? Some answers to these questions are provided in this chapter, dealing with employment and training programmes, and in the next chapter, dealing with non-claimant, non-employed status.

The previous chapter made extensive use of administrative data from the JUVOS system of computerised claimant histories. The more specific topics of this and subsequent chapters can only be addressed through the information obtained from the survey interviews. Respondents told us, at each interview, what their employment status had been, for each week over the preceding six months or so. This is our key information, since it permits us to calculate both how soon they made their moves into various types of status, and how long they spent in each status.

An initial break-down of time

It may be helpful, before looking at particular aspects, to have a broader picture of how time was divided between different types of status. This picture is supplied in Table 5.1.

The position up to the first survey interview

Since the week-by-week status data are so crucial, it is worth noting a few points about how they were used. In each survey interview, this material was collected from a fixed date, up to the time of the interview. Subsequently, we looked up the individual's start date of claim, counted forward 26 weeks, and discarded any status information from the first survey interview which preceded this date. Because the date of the first survey interview varied somewhat relative to the start of claim, the period covered after this treatment ranged

Table 5.1 Average proportions of time in various statuses, between Restart and the first and second survey interviews

column percentages (weighted)

| | to 1st interview | | to 2nd interview | |
	Control	Restart	Control	Restart
Unemployment (claiming)	72.5	65.9	58.8	54.4
Jobs or self-employment	19.3	21.1	23.2	27.4
ET or other programme	3.1	5.6	4.5	7.2
Full-time education/ training	0.3	0.6	1.7	1.2
Non-claimant, non-employed	4.9	6.4	11.8	9.7

Note: figures do not add to 100 per cent, by columns, because of small differences in the length of the reference period between individuals.

from 25 to 28 weeks. Those who took part in a further survey interview supplied a further block of information covering about another six months. There was by design a one-week overlap between the beginning of the second block and the end of the first, and this overlap was discarded from the second to form a continuous block for about one year, though with minor variations in length.

The first row of information in Table 5.1 has already been used in Chapter 4. It was pointed out there that these percentages at the second interview were compared with those derived from JUVOS records for the same period, and close agreement was found. This strengthens confidence in the quality of the information obtained from the interview material.

Our interest now is with the rest of the information in the table. It shows, first of all, the relative importance of the various outcomes apart from being unemployed. Employment, including self-employment, was by far the most important, accounting for about one fifth of time up to the first survey interview, and for about one quarter of time up to the second survey interview. The second most important was the non-claimant, non-employed status (including registered sickness), which accounted for about six per cent of time over the first six months and for about 10 per cent over the year. Employment Training (ET) and other government training programmes came a close third up to the first interview, having amounted to nearly six per cent of time up to then, but this percentage increased relatively little up to the time of the second survey interview. Finally, full-time education was the activity of a very small minority, accounting for little over one per cent of time in the year as a whole.

The comparisons between the control group and the Restart group in the table suggest several possible differences (the reliability of these will be statistically tested later).[1] Members of the control group spent slightly less time in employment or self-employment up to the first survey interview, and this gap had increased by the time of the second survey interview. So far as ET and other training programmes were concerned, the control group again spent less time in this status than the Restart group, the difference being about the same both in the first six months and over the whole year. In the case of non-claimant, non-employed status, the control group appeared to spend less time in the first half of the study period, but more time than the Restart group over the whole period. This last group will form the subject of the next chapter, but now we will consider whether the apparent differences concerning jobs and ET were statistically reliable.

Time in jobs and self-employment
As in the analysis of claiming in Chapter 4, we found it preferable to consider time in employment relative to previous employment experience.[2] The first survey interview supplied information for each of the previous five years (1984-88) of the numbers of months spent in jobs or self-employment. The clearest results were obtained by taking the middle three of those years (1985-87) together. The change in employment was measured as the difference between the percentage in the survey period, and the percentage in the 1985-87 period.

In that previous period of three years, the average percentage of time spent in employment had been 42 per cent. (This figure applied to both the control group and the Restart group). Employment up to the first survey interview was at just half this rate, 21 per cent, but increased considerably up to the second survey interview, when it stood at 27 per cent. Over either the shorter or the longer survey period, the change measure was a negative one. Such a negative figure does not indicate an historical worsening of the job market, but reflects the selection of the sample at a time when they would be faring relatively badly (having nearly completed six months of unemployment). The change or difference in employment can be interpreted as a measure of how far the sample was recovering from unemployment and returning to a more customary level of employment.

The analysis proceeded very much as in the case of change in claiming, which was described in the previous chapter. A multivariate analysis was carried out, with change in employment as the variable to be explained, and with the usual set of variables to explain it, including the control group versus Restart comparison (see Chapter 1 for details of explanatory variables). The analysis was carried out first for the six-month period up to the first survey interview, then for the one-year period to the second survey interview.[3]

The analysis for the first six months, based on 4,807 individuals, produced an estimate of the effect of Restart which was similar to the small difference indicated by Table 5.1, but this effect was shown to be, statistically, not significantly different from zero.[4] In the short-term, then, there was no distinct Restart effect on the time spent in employment.

It may be of interest briefly to note which were the main influences on this short-term outcome, as this has frequently been studied in previous research. The largest influences were those of age and family composition. Those aged under 25 spent the most time in jobs (relative to their previous employment), while this job outcome grew steadily less favourable with increasing age. So far as family structure was concerned, the most time was spent in jobs (relative to past employment) by those who were:

- married

- without young (under five) children

- but with dependent children.

It is interesting that the number of children in the family (which is also a good indicator of the level of state benefits received) was positively related to the proportion of time in employment. This relationship can, in a provisional way and subject to further research, be interpreted as 'need for increased income' predominating over 'availability of benefits'.

A possibly surprising finding was that those with driving licences, and (to a lesser degree) those with educational qualifications, tended to do less well in terms of this measure of employment. Remembering that this is a measure of change between two time periods, we tentatively suggest as an interpretation that, for this sample, qualification were currently of declining value in short-term job-search. This is a potentially important finding which differs from some previous evidence[5] and may merit further investigation.

Turning to the analysis for the full year after the Restart interview, it should first be noted that the sample had now been reduced to 3,419 and the control group had similarly shrunk to 186. This second analysis, which was specified similarly to the first,[6] gave some support to the existence of a Restart effect upon employment. However, the results were less clear-cut than in most other parts of our analysis. A significant Restart effect increasing the time spent in employment (relative to previous employment) was found, but this depended upon the way that the control group was defined (the only point in the study where control group specification made a substantial difference).[7]

This analysis must be regarded as inconclusive. In Chapter 7, however, we will return to the issue by examining somewhat more complex models of time spent in employment specifically during the second half of the study period. For the moment, we will turn to the evidence of analyses using a different type of job-related outcome measure.

Time to enter employment

Chapter 4 drew a distinction between the time spend as a claimant, and the (elapsed) time taken to exit from claimant status. Analogously, this chapter has looked at time spent in jobs or self-employment, and now looks at the time taken to enter into employed status. In other words, whereas in Chapter 4 we looked at the first exit from unemployment, we now look at the first move into employment, irrespective of whether that was from unemployment, from ET or other training programme, or from non-claimant status.

The statistical technique used is, as in Chapter 4, survival analysis.[8] This permits account to be taken of the fact that, for many people, no move into employment had taken place by the end of the period under consideration.

An initial analysis considered the time taken to move into jobs up to the time of the first survey interview. This suggested that Restart reduced the time taken to enter employment, but the finding was only

Fig. 5.1 Time for initial entry to employment

A. "Base case" respondent
B. Areas with highest labour turnover
C. Areas with lowest
D. Areas with greatest decline in unemployment
E. Areas with least
F. Earliest start of claim
G. Latest start
H. Aged 25-34
I. Aged 35-44
J. Aged 45-54
K. Aged 55 plus
L. Academic qualification
M. Vocational qualification
N. Single
O. 1 child under 5
P. 2+ children under 5
Q. Has driving licence
R. Health problem/disabled
S. 0% employed in 85-87
T. 100% employed in 85-87
U. Control group member

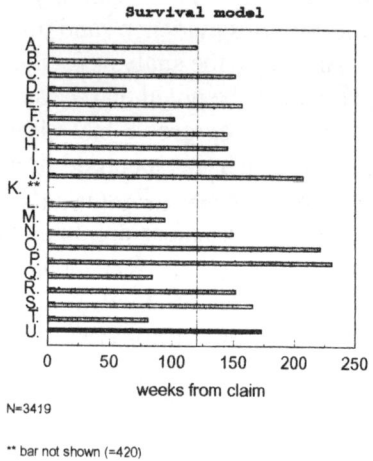

Survival model

N=3419

** bar not shown (=420)

(bar chart: weeks from claim, axis 0, 50, 100, 150, 200, 250; items A through U)

just significant.[9] We proceeded to apply the same form of analysis to the full one-year period of the study. The results of this analysis proved to be much more clear-cut than with the shorter time-period, and also by comparison with those described in the previous section of the chapter, relating to the proportion of time in employment. The Restart effect on 'time to enter employment' was estimated to be both large and highly significant.[10] To provide an impression of the relative size of all the significant influences in the model, they are shown in bar chart form in Figure 5.1. The 'base case' or reference person is indicated by the central vertical line in the figure, so that the effects of each influence can be assessed relative to this base case. The only variables with a larger influence upon time to enter employment were, being over 45, and having a young child, both of which greatly increased the average time.

The findings of the previous section of the chapter could only offer weak evidence of an effect of Restart upon the average proportion of time spent in employment (relative to a base-line period), but the present analysis suggests a rather large and significant effect from Restart upon time into employment. Indeed, being in the control group rather than the Restart group appeared to increase the average time into employment by around 25 per cent. There may seem to be some inconsistency here, but two considerations may help to reconcile the results of the different analyses. First, the earlier analysis did not give any special consideration to those who never entered employment during the study period. The survival analysis does treat these more satisfactorily, by fitting them into the overall distribution of times and in a sense extrapolating beyond the study period. By taking this into consideration, the survival analysis arrives at a view which may well be different from a regression analysis.

The second consideration is that the relation between time to enter employment, and proportion of time spent in employment, will depend upon the stability of the jobs obtained. If all jobs last for long periods, then the main differences in the individuals' proportions of times in employment (over a study period of only one year) will arise from how long it initially takes them to get into jobs. At the other extreme, if all jobs are very short-lived, with fairly substantial gaps between them, getting to a job early will make relatively much less difference to time spent in employment, since one will also tend to come out of the job earlier. The issue of the stability of jobs will be considered further at a later point in the chapter.

A further point requiring some discussion is the considerably clearer Restart effect upon time to enter employment, when the full one-year rather than initial six-month period of the study was considered. This may seem surprising, since it may suggest that the effects of Restart were delayed rather than rapid. On reflection, however, this may not be unreasonable. As Chapter 3 showed, the Restart interviews focused less often directly upon jobs and job search and more often upon entry to programmes such as ET, EAS or Jobclubs. It would often take some time for the effects of such programmes to show through in terms of entry to jobs.

Time in ET and other programmes
At the time of the survey, Employment Training (ET) was the chief programme of training available to people with six months or more of unemployment, although short Restart courses were also provided, as well as a variety of more specialised facilities (for example, for

disabled people). Because of the predominance of ET, we will use that label to cover all the periods spent by members of the sample on government programmes during the study period. As shown in Chapter 3, ET itself was one of the main possibilities discussed in Restart interviews, and one of the main areas where the Restart counsellor gave practical assistance to the unemployed person. It seemed likely that Restart would be stimulating entry to ET.

The proportion of time spent on government programmes in the five years prior to the study period (1984-88) was a little more than six per cent.[11] To make this figure more concrete, it represents one half of the sample having spent six months on a government programme over the period of five years. As the average age of the sample was young, much of this previous experience could have come through the Youth Training Scheme (YTS, now renamed YT).

As Table 5.1 has shown, the figure of six per cent of time on government programmes (in this case, chiefly ET) persisted over the one-year period of the study. Unlike the procedure with employment status, there seemed little point in comparing current level of participation in government programmes with previous levels. Earlier exploratory analyses (see Chapter 1) had shown that previous levels of participation in government programmes were not related to current outcomes. This is to be expected, both because of the variety of programmes on which people would previously have participated, and also because the present sample would not be representative of any programme. Further, the focusing of current resources on ET (still quite a new programme up to the time of the study), in many respects represented a new departure which might make comparisons with the past misleading.

We therefore measured participation in ET in absolute terms, rather than relative to past experience. For technical reasons, the analysis of participation up to the first survey interview was limited to considering 'any' ET participation against 'none' rather than considering it in percentage terms.[12] This analysis, which incorporated the usual set of explanatory variables, produced weak evidence of a positive effect of Restart upon participation in ET up to the first survey interview.[13] The use of a rather crude measure of ET participation may have contributed to this weak result.

Over the whole year of the study period, we were able to use the information about ET participation in a more satisfactory way,

**Fig. 5.2   Proportion of time spent in Employment
Training or other training**

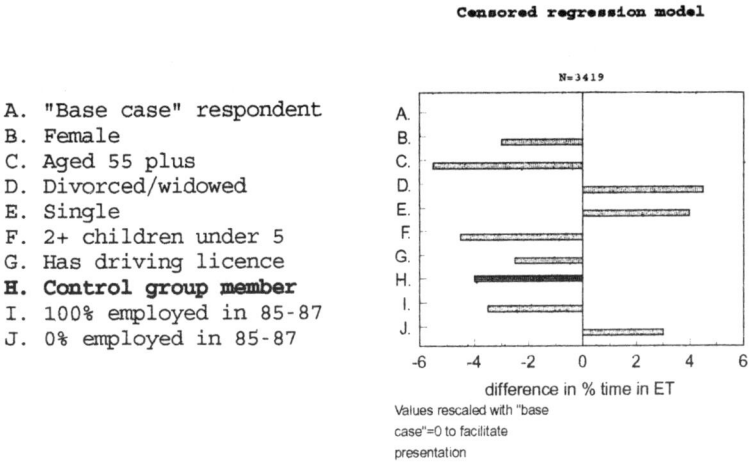

Censored regression model

N=3419

A. "Base case" respondent
B. Female
C. Aged 55 plus
D. Divorced/widowed
E. Single
F. 2+ children under 5
G. Has driving licence
H. **Control group member**
I. 100% employed in 85-87
J. 0% employed in 85-87

difference in % time in ET

Values rescaled with "base
case"=0 to facilitate
presentation

expressing it as a percentage of total time since the start of the study
period. Over this longer time-period, the Restart effect on ET
participation was found to be positive and clearly significant:[14]
members of the control spent, on average, a lower proportion of their
time on ET than did those passing through Restart.

It is of interest to consider the characteristics, apart from being
included in Restart, which were linked to spending a higher proportion
of time in ET. These were as follows:

• being male

• being less than 55 years old

• being single, separated or divorced

• having not more than one under-five child

• not having a driving licence

• having a relatively low level of recent job experience

These findings can be compared with those of Chapter 3, concerning the characteristics linked to ET being discussed as an option within the Restart interview. It appears that rather similar characteristics were important in both the focusing of Restart interviews upon ET, and participation in ET. In each instance factors associated with disadvantage in the job market seem to be important. Being married, having a driving licence, and having plenty of recent job experience are all factors which are helpful to getting jobs. The significant effects are summarised graphically in Figure 5.2.

Time to enter ET

A survival analysis of time to enter ET was developed along much the same lines as the survival analysis of entry to employment, described earlier in this chapter. We carried out the survival analysis both for the first six months of the study period and for the full year, as we expected to find more of an effect of Restart in the earlier period. In fact, there was little difference between the influences identified in the two analyses, so we will confine the account to the second, with its larger perspective.

This analysis showed that those in the control group took longer to get into ET than those passing through Restart.[15] It should be recalled that this calculation, in survival analysis, also takes into account those never entering ET during the study period, and their probability of ever doing so in the future. The Restart effect on entry-time to ET, though significant, was perhaps less marked than might have been expected. Part of the reason for this may be that the number of control group members going into ET was quite small, which makes it harder to get a statistically reliable estimate of the Restart effect. The size of the Restart effect on ET entry time which the model estimates is in fact quite large, but the confidence limits on it are wide. As a result the significance level of the Restart effect here is less than in the case of exit-time from unemployment (see Chapter 4) or of entry-time to employment (see above, this chapter).

The other significant influences upon entry-time to ET were almost the same as those which were important in explaining the proportion of time spent in ET. Accordingly, this analysis does not develop our interpretation in any important way, but tends to confirm the picture already obtained. The significant effects found in this analysis are summarised in Figure 5.3.

Fig. 5.3 **Estimated time to enter Employment Training or other training**

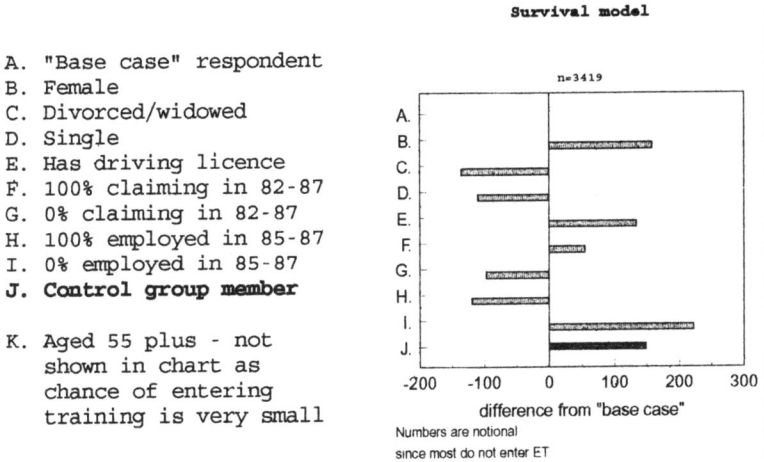

Survival model

A. "Base case" respondent
B. Female
C. Divorced/widowed
D. Single
E. Has driving licence
F. 100% claiming in 82-87
G. 0% claiming in 82-87
H. 100% employed in 85-87
I. 0% employed in 85-87
J. **Control group member**

K. Aged 55 plus - not shown in chart as chance of entering training is very small

n=3419

difference from "base case"
Numbers are notional since most do not enter ET

To conclude this section, there was clearly a Restart effect upon ET entry and participation, but perhaps of a smaller magnitude than might have been expected. Some commentators have suggested that Restart has largely had a 'register effect', moving people either into inactivity or onto government programmes but not at all or very little into jobs. However, the findings of this study indicate that the effects of Restart in stimulating movement into ET were of a similar size to its effects in stimulating movement into jobs. In both cases, moreover, the effects became considerably clearer over the course of a year, than over the course of the first six months after Restart. This seems more consistent with a cumulative impact from the numerous different programmes and services into which Restart feeds, and inconsistent with the notion of a direct or immediate 'push' from Restart itself.

The quality of jobs after unemployment
The assessment of the time-related effects of Restart upon employment and upon participation in government programmes has

now been completed. There remain a number of issues concerning the nature or 'quality' of jobs entered by the sample. These issues are of interest for three reasons.

- First, as discussed earlier in the chapter, there is the possibility that a high incidence of jobs which are short-lived will tend to limit the total effect of Restart.

- Second, as noted in Chapter 1, the most common outcome used in labour market evaluation research has been change in the individual wage level, a measure of job quality.

- Third, some commentators have suggested that Restart, through its eligibility checks, puts pressures upon unemployed people to take jobs which are of low quality. If true, this might suggest that any advantage of Restart in stimulating early entry to jobs may be offset by longer-term losses (such as through low utilisation of human capital).

Job stability. We will first of all consider job stability. Although little considered in much research on unemployment, it is an aspect of obvious importance both for individuals and for policy. Job stability, for individuals, represents security. For policy, a high level of stability in new jobs after unemployment represents not only more satisfied clients, but also lower recurrent costs of benefit payments and placement and support services.

Stability can be assessed in different ways, which do not necessarily yield the same results. One simple approach, in the present study, is to consider those people who were employed at the first-stage survey interview, and identify what proportion of these were also employed at the second-stage survey interview six months later. For those with full-time jobs at stage one, 76 per cent were in some kind of employment at stage two. For those with part-time jobs at stage one (defined as 8-29 hours per week), the proportion employed six months later was 82 per cent, and for those initially in self-employment, the proportion was 90 per cent. These figures seem to indicate quite a high level of stability, but the picture is a biased one. At any one time, those with longer-lasting jobs will necessarily be over-represented while those with shorter jobs will be under-represented. For instance, many of those with short-lived jobs will have been employed *before* the first survey interview, or *between* the first and the second, but not be employed at either survey interview.

An alternative approach is to consider jobs rather than individuals. There are several complications, however: one person can have several jobs over a period, a job can either have ended or be continuing when the study period comes to an end, and jobs obtained late in the study period will be more likely to be incomplete at the end. It is difficult to get a complete picture without making it too complex to be useful.

After some experimentation, we found that a helpful picture could be obtained by defining two classes of jobs and concentrating solely on those. To begin with, we confine our attention to those in the study who were interviewed twice, because it was only for these that we had a sufficiently long period to assess stability. For these, we first identified the initial job obtained in the study period, *provided that* it had also come to an end in the study period. The second class of jobs identified consisted of any job that was still continuing at the end of the study period (whether it was the first or a later job obtained by the individual). These two classes are mutually exclusive. They also accounted for a little more than 90 per cent of all jobs. The only jobs excluded are those which were neither initial jobs nor continuing at the end of the study period. Naturally, these will virtually all be short-lived jobs, so that they can be taken into account quite easily.

Table 5.2 shows the relative size of the two defined classes of jobs, and presents the average length of the jobs in each class. (This is done separately for full-time, part-time, and self-employed jobs.) It should be appreciated, of course, that the average durations of the continuing jobs only go to the end of the study period and so considerably understate the true (completed) averages. They nevertheless help to establish the contrast between the two classes of jobs which we have defined.

Evidently, the initial jobs which have been completed on average represented much less stable jobs than those which were continuing at the end of the study period. The initial completed jobs lasted about 13 weeks if they were jobs as employees, and 16 weeks if they were self-employed jobs. The incomplete jobs had already on average continued for about twice as long as this, by the end of the study period.

So the relative proportions of initial and completed jobs provide a simple indicator of the general level of job stability. Table 5.2 shows that on this basis at least 40 per cent of all jobs obtained were short-lived or unstable. Clearly, then, there was a considerable degree

Table 5.2 Indicators of the stability of jobs

	Employed		Self-
	Full-time	Part-time	employed
a) Initial completed jobs			
- mean duration (weeks)	13.3	13.4	16.1
- number of jobs	533	193	66
- % of all jobs	41	37	26
b) Continuing jobs			
- mean incomplete duration (weeks)	27.9	25.7	29.0
- number of jobs	696	280	186
- % of all jobs	54	54	74
Total jobs	1301	516	252

of instability in the jobs, taken as a whole. A much higher degree of stability, however, was being achieved by the relatively small proportion of the sample who were going into self-employment. Only one-quarter of these moves into self-employment proved to be short-lived, while three-quarters were continuing at the end of the study period.

Were there any indications that Restart was connected with getting stable jobs more (or less) frequently? Here, as with other aspects of job quality, the potential for analysis is limited by the small size of the control group. This means that we cannot look separately at full-time, part-time and self-employed jobs in making this comparison: it is necessary to pool across the three groups (and we still only have about 80 jobs in the control group to base the analyses upon). So far as this analysis takes us, it shows no indication of a difference between the control group and the Restart participants. Some 41 per cent of the jobs held by the control group were initial jobs that had been completed, while the corresponding proportion for the Restart group was 40 per cent.

In terms of the stability measure, therefore, there was no indication that Restart was leading to people taking less stable jobs; or conversely, there was no indication that when left out of Restart, people were able to find jobs of greater stability. The fairly high general prevalence of short-lived jobs does, however, indicate a likely external constraint or limit upon the functioning of Restart or similar programmes.

Wages. There is no a priori reason to expect a Restart effect upon wages in one direction or another. It is not part of the aims of Restart to influence the wages obtained by individuals in their new jobs, although the aims do include the encouragement of effective job search, which will involve various issues concerning wages. Restart could for example encourage people to reduce their idea of the lowest wage which they would consider, or could conversely raise their self-confidence in their ability to apply for better-paid jobs.

Problems of control group sample size restricted what one could do in terms of a wage analysis. We had to put aside hopes of carrying out a full multivariate analysis to establish whether there was a Restart effect upon wages, because the wage data for the control group was too limited to bear the weight of such a sophisticated approach.[16] In fact, even at the first stage interview with its larger sample size, complete data on wages and hours of work in new jobs was available for only 46 control group members. We therefore limit ourselves to presenting descriptive statistics, which are shown in Table 5.3.

Table 5.3   Pay in jobs at the first interview stage

	Control group	Restart groups
Average weekly pay*	89.74	94.30
Average hourly pay*	2.83	2.74
Average weekly hours	32.7	34.5
Sample size+	46	1008

* as at September-November 1989

\+ those reporting both pay and hours data

At first sight it seems that the Restart group had achieved a lead of five per cent in terms of their earnings in their new jobs. But if one looks at hourly rates rather than weekly earnings, the picture is reversed, with the control group earning three per cent more per hour. The difference between the hourly and the weekly comparisons arises because the control group worked shorter hours on average, by nearly six per cent, relative to the Restart group. The Restart group may, one might think, have had somewhat better success in getting into full-time jobs. However, no such interpretation is really justifiable, because all the apparent differences in the table fall far short of statistical significance. The only safe conclusion is that there is no real evidence of differences in the wages and hours of new jobs between the groups.

The analysis, therefore, so far as it goes, suggests that Restart had no influence on wages at the individual level. The overall picture provided by the descriptive statistics of wages are mainly of interest in helping to identify the section of the job market into which this sample of unemployed people was moving. In 1989, the average hourly wage rate for all adult manual workers in Great Britain was £4.94, nearly 80 per cent above the average rate achieved by the present sample. Some further information about wages, relating to expectations or targets rather than achieved wages, will be presented in Chapter 7.

Occupational group of new jobs. In order to complete this brief outline of 'job quality' after unemployment, we will consider one other indicator. This is the occupational group of the new jobs. It was, once again, not part of Restart's aims to influence the occupational group in which unemployed people sought jobs. However, there might be some incidental effects, although there is no strong reason for supposing these to operate in one direction or another. In addition, descriptive information about occupations before and after the focal unemployment claim increases understanding of the job market context in which Restart was operating at the time. Finally, there is considerable interest among labour market analysts in how unemployment may affect occupational mobility; the descriptive information should be of relevance to these interests, although we do not take the analysis very far.

The occupational codes, for all the jobs covered in the survey interviews, were translated into the Goldthorpe Class Schema. This divides jobs into 11 categories, which can also be collapsed into a simplified grouping of three broad levels: higher occupations or 'service class' (broadly speaking, the professional and corporate management level); intermediate occupational class (consisting largely of routine white-collar, lower technician, and supervisory jobs, and small proprietors); and the lower occupational class (manual and personal service workers). Some adaptations of the scheme place female routine white-collar workers in the lower occupational class.

Some information has already been given, in Chapter 2, about the occupational origins of the sample. Here we are chiefly interested in examining the general distribution of the new jobs, and whether this represented a different or a similar distribution to what had come before.

A problem in making such comparisons lies in a feature of the previous work histories which has been highlighted in Chapter 2. Many people had not had previous jobs, or had last held a job so long ago that it would not be sensible to use it as a benchmark of the person's position in the labour market prior to the current period of unemployment. To calculate the prior distribution of occupations, there are two main options. One is to exclude those without reasonably recent prior jobs from the distribution altogether. This comes to the same thing as assuming that they would have the same occupational distribution as for the rest of the sample, if only one could observe it. The other approach is to count them as part of the lower occupational group, on the grounds that their lack of recent job experience means that they can only hope to get work of a low skill-level. On balance, it seems a less drastic assumption to leave them out of the calculations.

The comparison needed is between the previous jobs and the new jobs of those who were in new jobs at the time of the survey (we take

Table 5.4   Occupational level of new and previous jobs

	New jobs	Previous jobs
Higher level	9 %	13 %
Intermediate level	33 %	30 %
Lower level	58 %	57 %

Base: all in jobs at first survey interview, and providing occupational information the first survey interview because it yields slightly large numbers). There were 64 control group members who were in a job at this time and provided enough information for their jobs to be coded. This small number compels us to carry out the analysis only at the broadest level, that is, with the three-class schema of occupations.

First, Table 5.4 above shows the overall distribution of jobs, comparing new with previous.

The new jobs were distributed in a closely similar way to the previous jobs; apparent small differences in the table are statistically non-significant. There is no evidence here of a progressive down-grading of occupational levels, as some previous research on unemployed samples has found.[17]

When this comparison was repeated with the individuals' longest-duration prior jobs (rather than with the most recent prior jobs), a very similar picture emerged, so the details are not shown here. This result was as would be expected, given the fact that the occupational levels of the longest and the most recent jobs were very similar for the whole sample.

Comparisons were then made between the control group members and Restart participants, within those who were in a job at the first stage survey interview. Once more the differences were small, and

Table 5.5 Occupational levels of Restart and control group members

	Control group	Restart groups
a) New jobs (post-unemployment)		
Higher level	6 %	10 %
Intermediate level	30 %	34 %
Lower level	64 %	57 %
b) Previous jobs		
Higher level	11 %	13 %
Intermediate level	24 %	30 %
Lower level	65 %	57 %

Base: all in jobs at first survey interview, and providing occupational information statistically non-significant, so there was no indication of any effect of Restart upon occupational groupings. However, the results are summarised in Table 5.5 above, largely for the sake of descriptive completeness.

Not only was there not much difference between the distributions of the control and Restart groups, but each group had maintained a very similar distribution of occupations from before to after unemployment.

Summary of chapter
The main findings of the chapter have been that Restart exerted significant effects both upon individuals' employment and upon their participation in ET and other programmes (all treated as one group).

These effects were not large, and for them to become fully apparent required the full year of follow-up information after the initial Restart interview. The clearest effects concerned entry time into jobs and ET, with Restart participants having clearly shorter times on average compared with control group members. Restart participants also spent a larger proportion of the study period in ET, but evidence about the proportion of time spent in jobs (which was measured relative to employment in a baseline period) was inconclusive.

We went on to consider three indicators of job quality: stability of jobs, wages, and occupational level. There was no evidence of a Restart effect, one way or the other, on any of these indicators. This is consistent with the aims of Restart, which are neutral in these respects. However, we were only able to carry out rather simple analyses, because of the small numbers of control group members in jobs. It remains possible that significant differences have been obscured because of this.

The descriptive findings for the unemployed sample as a whole may be of some interest. The main descriptive points were that at least 40 per cent of new jobs were short-lived, average wages were at a little more than half the average for manual workers, and the occupational distribution of the new jobs (as of jobs held before the recent period of unemployment) was skewed away from higher occupations and towards lower occupations. These findings are broadly consistent with the findings of previous research on unemployment.

The short-lived nature of many of the jobs obtained by people after six months of unemployment is, probably, the most relevant descriptive finding in relation to Restart. While the findings presented earlier in the chapter showed a particularly clear Restart effect, in terms of reducing the average time taken to get into jobs, some of the potential advantage will be lost if the job lasts only a short time, as was the case with many of the jobs for this sample.

Even a short-lived job may well be much better than no job at all; a short-lived job may also be a stepping-stone towards a more regular job at a later stage; and any period of employment is likely to contribute both to the financial wellbeing of the individual and to the economy and exchequer. Further, there is no evidence that Restart itself fosters short-lived jobs. The point is, rather, that the prevalence of short-lived jobs places a constraint on what can be achieved by a service like Restart. Conversely, under conditions of greater employment stability, the effect of Restart on individual employment would tend to be greater.

6 Non-claimant, Non-employed Status

People who leave the unemployment register for outcomes other than employment, education or training are an under-researched group. Much of the background knowledge which can be assumed in the case of unemployed or employed groups is lacking for these. Accordingly, the balance of this chapter is somewhat different to the two previous chapters. First, for the sake of continuity with the previous chapters, we present the findings from our usual multivariate statistical analyses, to test for a Restart effect on movements into this status. After that, however, we develop a more detailed descriptive account with particular attention to the reasons for the movements. Partly, the aim in developing this account is to help fill the gap in existing knowledge, for a large group with considerable importance for policy issues. But this descriptive account is also more directly relevant to the aims of this study. Various commentators have surmised that Restart has a large effect in moving people off the register but *not* into employment or training. We in contrast will show that the Restart effect in this respect is quite moderate, and short-lived. Because of this possibly surprising result, it becomes particularly important to have a better understanding of this group and of the influences which form it.

Definitions

There is no convenient word of phrase to define the group as a whole. We could refer to them accurately as 'non-employed non-claimants' but this would soon seem tedious. For the sake of convenience, people who are not in work, education or training and are not signing on as unemployed will be referred to here by the shorthand term 'non-claimants'. This accords with with the 'claimant count' definition of unemployment. There is little risk of 'non-claimants' being confused with those in jobs or on programmes. However, we shall also make reference to the commonly used measure of 'economic inactivity' based upon the ILO/OECD definition of unemployment, used in the Labour Force Survey.

Under the ILO/OECD definition, the following groups are defined as unemployed: claimants and non-claimants who were seeking work within the previous four weeks and who would be available to start work within two weeks, plus those who are waiting to start a new job already obtained. By this definition most importantly, non-claimants who have been seeking work or who are waiting to start a job are considered as unemployed rather than economically inactive. Conversely, those not seeking employment during the reference period, and not currently in employment, are by the ILO/OECD formula defined as being economically inactive.

The ILO/OECD definition of inactivity overlaps with the 'non-claimant' group defined here, but many non-claimants identified by the survey were, in fact, continuing to seek employment though no longer claiming. This is shown in Table 6.1 which reports the proportions with various levels of job applications.

Table 6.1   Job applications* for 'non-claimants' and others at the time of the first survey interview

Column percentages

Frequency of applications	'Non-claimants'	Others
None	39	16
1-5	34	34
6-10	19	34
11-19	4	9
20+	3	7
N (unweighted)	509	4289

*   In the four-week reference period.

Overall, the level of job applications was much lower among 'non-claimants' than among the remainder. However, on the ILO/OECD definition, only 39 per cent would definitely be classified as 'inactive', while the remaining 61 per cent would be classified as 'unemployed' provided that they would be available for work.

Time spent in 'non-claimant' status

As Table 5.1 in the previous chapter showed, 'non-claimant' status accounted for a substantial proportion of time both in the first six months of the study period and over the full year: around six per cent and 10 per cent respectively. There were also some apparent differences between the control group and Restart group members, but these changed direction between the shorter-term and the longer-term measure. Initially, the control group appeared to spend less time in 'non-claimant' status, but later this seemed to be reversed. Our first task is to assess the statistical reliability of these differences.

Time in 'non-claimant' status was measured in absolute terms, not relative to prior level; apart from other considerations, the survey gathered no direct information about the latter. The measure came from individuals' recall of their employment status, week by week, from the commencement of the study period (see Chapter 5 for further details). Weeks in 'non-claimant' status were expressed as a percentage of the period of the status record being considered, which would vary slightly in length between individuals.

The usual set of variables, including 'control group versus Restart', were put to work to account for time in the 'non-claimant' status. A significant Restart effect was confirmed for the initial six-month period. Control group members spent less time in 'non-claimant' status, so that Restart was tending to increase the time spent in this status.[1]

The effect of Restart was relatively small by comparison with three other, very marked influences upon time in 'non-claimant' status. Since much of the later analysis will focus upon these three influences, it is worth noting them now:

• gender: women on average spent a larger proportion of time in 'non-claimant' status than men.

• young children: those with any children aged under five tended to spend substantially higher proportions of time in 'non-claimant' status.

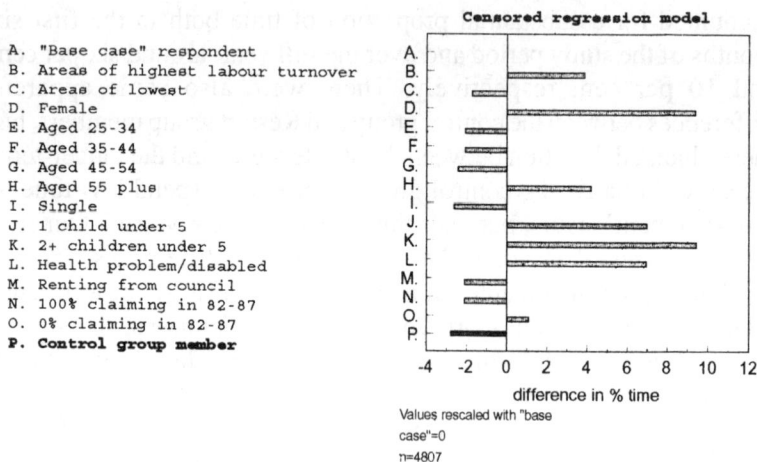

Fig. 6.1 Proportion of "non-claimant" time in period from 6-12 months after unemployment claim

Censored regression model

A. "Base case" respondent
B. Areas of highest labour turnover
C. Areas of lowest
D. Female
E. Aged 25-34
F. Aged 35-44
G. Aged 45-54
H. Aged 55 plus
I. Single
J. 1 child under 5
K. 2+ children under 5
L. Health problem/disabled
M. Renting from council
N. 100% claiming in 82-87
O. 0% claiming in 82-87
P. Control group member

difference in % time

Values rescaled with "base case"=0
n=4807

- disability or ill-health: those stating that they were affected by these problems also tended to spend high proportions of time in 'non-claimant' status.

The analysis was repeated for those completing a second survey interview. In this longer period, the Restart effect shifted from positive to negative, although by the usual criteria applied in this study the difference was not significant.[2] This outcome contrasts with the findings of the previous chapter, where the Restart effect upon both employment and upon participation in ET tended to get more pronounced in the longer time-period.

The three major effects on 'non-claimant' status, which were highlighted above, continued to be as important in the longer period as they had been in the shorter. In the longer period, moreover, being aged over 55 became highly important, although it had a relatively minor effect over the initial six months.

The significant effects identified at the first survey are shown graphically in Figure 6.1, while those identified at the second survey,

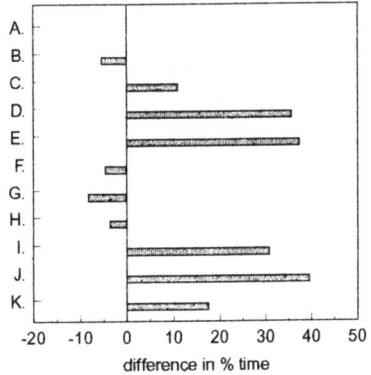

Fig. 6.2 Proportion of "non-claimant" in period
from 6-18 months after unemployment claim

Censored regression model

A. "Base case" respondent
B. Areas with greatest
decline in unemployment
C. Areas with least
D. Female
E. Aged 55 plus
F. Vocational qualification
G. Single
H. 1 child
I. 1 child under 5
J. 2+ children under 5
K. Health problem/disabled

difference in % time

Values rescaled with "base
case"=0

N=3419

Note: Control group not
significantly different
from Restart group

and relating to the whole study period, are shown in Figure 6.2. The
control group is not included in Figure 6.2, since the Restart effect in
this case was not significant.

Time to enter 'non-claimant' status

A survival analysis of time to enter 'non-claimant' status (for the first
time) was carried out much as for time to enter employment, or enter
ET, reported in Chapter 5. The analysis in the present case was
confined to the data covering the full one-year period of the study.

This proved to be an aspect where the estimates were sensitive to
the definitions and specifications used.[3] On balance, it would be
prudent to conclude that the Restart effect was not reliably different
from zero; but if anything, the tendency would be for Restart to
increase entry-times to non-employed status. This was much as
expected. We have already seen, using a different outcome measure,
that the Restart effect on 'non-claimant' status was a short-term one.
Survival analysis, on the other hand, gives full weight to longer-term

outcomes, by taking account of those who, at the end of the survey period, have never moved into this status. Gender, age, the presence of young children, and disability or ill-health appeared once more as the main factors in this analysis.

'Early exits' revisited

In Chapter 4 we examined the possibility that Restart might have some special effect in moving some people off the employment register at a very early stage. This could perhaps take place by voluntary withdrawal of claim, when faced with a Restart interview, and in that case 'non-claimant' status might be adopted instead. The earlier analysis showed that a specifically early effect only applied to women. We have now confirmed that women were particularly likely to move into a 'non-claimant' status, a finding already well known from previous research. Putting these points together, we surmise that the early effect of Restart upon women's claiming will particularly lead into a 'non-claimant' status.

We examined the distribution of times of moving into 'non-claimant' status, for men and women who were interviewed at the second stage of the survey.[4] Table 6.2 below charts the times up to the median for the two groups. It can be seen that the five-percentile time for women (that is, the time which was shorter than 95 per cent of the times) was six weeks, while the corresponding time for men was substantially larger, at 10 weeks. This difference gradually decreased across higher percentiles, so that by the time the median was reached, there was only one week's difference between women and men. The analysis does tend to confirm, therefore, that there was a larger cluster of women leaving the register early on, to go into 'non-claimant' status than in the case of men. But, it should be stressed, these differences

Table 6.2 Percentiles of exit times into non-claimant status, by gender

						Percentiles
	5	10	20	30	40	50
Men	10	14	19	25	29	32
Women	6	11	15	22	27	31

Note: Each entry is 'weeks from six months of claim'.

applied to quite small proportions of the total. One quarter of the total sample moved into 'non-claimant' status at some time, and if the difference between men and women applies chiefly among the first one-third of these to leave the register, then we are essentially talking about eight per cent or so of the sample. So, in clarifying an 'early exit' tendency among women, we have also confirmed that it was quite a small element in the overall picture.

It should also be stressed that the Restart effect upon movement into 'non-claimant' status was *not* confined either to an 'early exit' effect nor to a specifically 'female' effect. Using the same method of plotting percentiles of exit times, but this time for the Restart and control groups, we found (by comparison with the analysis by gender) larger differences which persisted longer over time. This is shown in Table 6.3.

Table 6.3   Percentiles of exit time into 'non-claimant' status, for the control group and Restart group

					Percentiles
	10	20	30	40	50
Control	16	25	30	32	37
Restart	12	17	23	28	31

In short, the Restart effect upon movement into non-activity seems to be quite clearly marked for the whole of the first six months of the study period, before being reversed in the second six months. Much of the remainder of this chapter will be concerned with understanding the wider changes in the position of the sample, which may help to explain this finding.

Further descriptive analysis of 'non-claimant' status
The rather short-term effects of Restart upon moves into 'non-claimant' status may seem surprising. They may seem still more surprising when the scale of such movements is fully appreciated. In fact, movement into this status comes close behind employment as a form of outflow from unemployment. At the time of the second survey interview, 16 per cent of respondents were 'non-claimants', but by this

time 26 per cent spent some time in this status over the period. Given that there is so much movement into this status, why does Restart not exert *more* influence in that direction? The answer may be that the *movements into 'non-claimant' status are already strongly controlled by other influences*. The chief influences have already been introduced earlier in this chapter. We will now develop a more detailed descriptive analysis of their operation.

In the following sections, the tables are presented (unlike in other parts of this report) in unweighted form. The main reason for this is that, with more detailed tables, we sometimes have small numbers in cells, and weighting can then become awkward or confusing. In any case, the patterns which will be described are so clearly marked that the minor differences introduced by weighting are hardly relevant.

Combinations of circumstances. The influences already highlighted are gender, the presence of young children, disability or ill-health, and age. These factors combine in certain ways to provide still more marked influences.

Differences in rates of 'non-claimant' status between men and women in the survey existed only for those aged under 40. Overall, twice as high a proportion of women as of men in the sample experienced 'non-claimant' status, but three times as many in the under-40 age groups.

After age was controlled for, the presence of children made no difference to male 'non-claimant' proportions, but women with children under five years old were more than twice as likely as other

Table 6.4 Women's experience of 'non-claimant' status by presence and age of children

	Percentage experiencing 'non-claimant' status	
	%	BASE
Women with children under 5	40	(477)
Women with children aged 5 to 16, but no under 5s	19	(90)
Women with no children under 16	16	(1123)

women to be 'non-claimants'. Having children between five and fifteen years of age only increased women's proportion in 'non-claimant' status very slightly when there were no children younger than five in the same household (Table 6.4).

Problems of health or disability appeared to have some influence on women's tendency to enter 'non-claimant' status, but only after reaching the age of 25. Among men, disability or ill-health was perhaps *the* major influence on becoming 'non-claimant', at all ages, but it grew markedly more important between 40 and 60. This is shown in Table 6.5.

Table 6.5   Percentage of 'non-claimants' with a health problem or disability, by age within gender

Men	'Non-claimant' at some stage		Never 'non-claimant'	
Age	%	BASE	%	BASE
16-24	33	(95)	22	(1030)
25-39	49	(102)	31	(1117)
40-49	75	(56)	42	(476)
50-59	82	(67)	55	(385)

Women	'Non-claimant' at some time		Never 'non-claimant'	
Age	%	BASE	%	BASE
16-24	28	(130)	28	(447)
25-39	33	(169)	24	(494)
40-59	65	(74)	58	(368)

These analyses, taken in conjunction, suggest that one pattern increasing 'non-claimant' status, among unemployed women, is the case of pre-school children in the prime years of life, while for unemployed men, the predisposing factor to this status is disability or ill-health coupled with advancing age.

For women, the financial feasibility of moving into 'non-claimant' status during the early child-rearing years may depend largely upon having a husband or partner who is employed. In fact, those with partners working 24 hours a week or more are ineligible for income support, so that their claim is relatively unlikely to continue beyond 12 months of unemployment (when unemployment benefit comes to an end). Consistent with this, we found (at the second survey interview) that 63 per cent of 'non-claimant' women had partners who were working full-time, while this applied to just nine per cent of 'non-claimant' men. This type of asymmetry between the movements of men and women, in and out of claimant status, has generally been explained as a combination of the effect of lower wages for women, and of differences in the acceptability of economically dependant roles.

For men, the financial feasibility of moving into 'non-claimant' status will depend partly on access to other benefits, notably income support on the basis of sickness or invalidity, and partly on the existence of pensions or other sources of personal income. Because sickness and disability are important reasons for 'non-claimant' status for men, they have relatively good chances of maintaining, or indeed improving, their benefit position as they cease to sign as unemployed. For the majority of women, on the other hand, ceasing to sign results from loss of eligibility, or recognition of ineligibility, and access to benefits is ended.

To illustrate this, as well as for other reasons, we produced a three-part categorisation of reasons for leaving the register, based on the benefit positions of people who were 'non-claimant' at the second survey interview (Table 6.6).

Category one comprised people who were known to be ineligible for benefit, either because they were living with a partner who was working full-time (the case for the majority of women) or because they declared benefit ineligibility as their reason for leaving the register. Category two comprised people who were not required to sign on in order to claim income support, and those who were receiving another type of benefit such as sickness benefit or a pension. This category included all those who left the unemployment register for reasons of sickness, disability, or caring responsibilities (unless they had already been placed in category one because they had a working partner). Category three comprised people whose benefit position was unclear. We can see from the table that men were concentrated in category two,

Table 6.6   Benefit eligibility groups, by gender

	Men %	Women %	All 'non-claimants' %
1. Ineligible for IS and not on sickness benefit	19	66	44
2. Entitled to IS without signing on or known to be receiving another benefit	67	25	44
3. Benefit position unclear	14	9	12
BASE	(270)	(313)	(583)

Note: IS = Income Support

mainly because of the large number who were receiving sickness benefit or pensions, whereas women were concentrated in category one, because a high proportion of them lived with employed partners.

These interpretations can be tested to some extent by other survey information. Reasons for leaving the register were given by respondents themselves at each of the two survey interviews. These were wide-ranging but can be grouped into six categories:

• about to take up a job, scheme or course

• retired

• sick or disabled

• having caring responsibilities or family problems

• financial and benefit reasons, including non-eligibility for benefits

• vague or 'other reasons' cited by only a small number of people, such as being away from home, in prison, settling in to a new area, or doing voluntary work.

The reasons of particular interest at this point are those concerning sickness or disablement, 73 per cent of which were given *by men*; and those concerning financial or benefit reasons, 62 per cent of which were given *by women*. The further breakdown of these reasons for ceasing to sign on is shown in Table 6.7.

Table 6.7   Detailed types of (a) sickness/disablement reasons, and (b) financial/benefit reasons, for 'non-claimant status'

(a) Sick/disabled

	1st interview %	2nd interview %
On sickness benefit	49	62
Temporary health problem/injury	9	6
Long-term/chronic health problem	9	18
Unspecified health problem	32	13
Registered disabled	1	-
Other health problem/disability	1	1

(b) Financial and benefit reasons

	1st interview %	2nd interview %
Ineligible for benefit	17	20
No longer eligible for benefit	48	55
Voluntary redundancy	1	2
Not required to sign on	8	9
Not yet signed on again	7	5
Other financial reason	20	10

In fact, benefit-related items were predominant in both sets of reasons. Especially by the second survey interview, those (chiefly men) who spoke of sickness or disability as their reason were generally moving onto sickness benefit. Financial and benefits reasons for 'non-claimant' status (given chiefly by women) focused chiefly on ineligibility, and again this grew more pronounced by the second interview.

These results are of considerable help towards explaining why Restart tends to stimulate movements into 'non-claimant' status during the first phase of the study, but not the second. As time goes on, the existing systems and structures of benefit increasingly influence movement into 'non-claimant' status, whether by choice or by constraint, so that in the second half of the study period, there is much less scope for Restart to have an *additional* influence. In particular, it is between six and 12 months of claiming (corresponding to the first half of the study period) that women who have an entitlement to unemployment benefit may, nonetheless, decide to move into a 'non-claimant' status. This is primarily influenced by the existence of child-care responsibility, or the advent of pregnancy, but the Restart procedures can also exert an influence. After 12 months of unemployment, women with full-time working husbands *in any case* lose their eligibility for benefit.

Similarly, in the case of men, Restart may early on assist movement towards a 'non-claimant' status for those with illnesses; at a later stage, the process of adjustment has largely been completed.

Employment and 'non-claimant' status
This discussion has so far centred upon the most obvious reasons for 'non-claimant' status. The connections between this status and employment are perhaps less obvious, and are certainly less important, but they are substantial and should not be ignored. In fact, as Table 6.8 below shows, at the first survey interview spells of 'non-claimant' before starting a job were as prominent a reason as caring responsibilities.

It does not seem entirely sensible to miss signing for benefits just because a job or course is about to start. But this should not, in most cases, be thought of as ceasing to sign after a claim, as only one in four were signing on immediately before becoming 'non-claimants'. About 40 per cent were in a full-time job and 20 per cent in a part-time job. 'Non-claimant' spells of this kind, therefore, seem linked to short-lived jobs. About two-thirds of those giving this reason for 'non-claimant' status were under-35, and two-thirds again were women. Most of the other groups going into 'non-claimant' status did so directly from an unemployed claim, and very few from employment.

When we compare reasons given at the second interview with those given at the first, the most notable change is the decrease in the proportion of people who left the register because they were about to

Table 6.8   Reasons for ceasing to sign as unemployed ('non-claimants' who were respondents to both survey interviews)

	1st interview %	2nd interview %
About to start job etc.	18	4
Retired	3	7
Sick/disabled	28	26
Carer	18	20
Financial/benefit reasons	25	34
Other reasons	8	9
BASE	(366)	(583)

start a job, scheme or course. There is clearly a duration effect causing the decrease in this category: those most likely to find jobs quickly will have done so in the early part of the year which we are looking at, leaving behind, as the year goes on, those who take longer to find jobs.

A further distinguishing feature of those becoming 'non-claimant' because of forthcoming jobs or courses, was that their spells in that status were short. Only 14 per cent lasted 17 or more weeks, to be compared with 74 per cent of those with financial or benefit reasons, 90 per cent for those with illness or disablement reasons, 96 per cent for carers, and 100 per cent for those who considered themselves retired.

Different forms of 'non-claimant' status were also related to previous employment histories. Table 6.9 shows what proportions of time had been spent in employment, over the past five years, by various types of 'non-claimants'. It suggests that the level of past employment can be an important condition for entry to 'non-claimant' status of some types.

Table 6.9   Reasons for leaving the register, by percentage of time spent in employment in the last 5 years

		Time in employment				
	None	<25 %	25-49 %	50-74 %	75- %	BASE
About to start job etc.	12	9	21	18	39	(98)
Retired	8	4	10	7	71	(48)
Sick/disabled	24	15	17	19	26	(191)
Carer	14	8	17	21	40	(144)
Financial/benefit reasons	8	9	9	20	55	(253)
Other reasons	17	12	15	17	39	(41)

Base: 'Non-claimant' at either first or second survey interview

This is clearly illustrated by the two largest sub-groups of 'non-claimants'. Those becoming 'non-claimants' because of illness or disability generally had low levels of prior employment: one quarter with no job in the past five years, and one quarter with a job most of the time. Many in this group had obviously already moved to the margins of the labour market before beginning their current period of unemployment. Those becoming 'non-claimants' for financial or benefit reasons, on the other hand, generally had good employment records over the previous five years. Their good work record may provide them with some additional financial resources for their change of status.

Financial circumstances in 'non-claimant' status
The Restart process has been shown to increase the proportion moving into 'non-claimant' status, in the period between six and 12 months after start of an unemployment claim. Concern has sometimes been expressed by labour market commentators that such movements off the register may cause additional hardship to some of those affected. The study did not collect very detailed information about the material and financial circumstances of the sample, but some indicators were

obtained. To complete this chapter, we consider this evidence about the relative circumstances of those moving into 'non-claimant' status.

We were able to compare the three different groupings of 'non-claimant' men and women (using the classification shown in Table 6.6) with three other groupings – working, students and unemployed – using two measures of financial circumstances. The first measure related to credit and debt: whether they had found it necessary to borrow money in the six months before the second survey interview, and whether, in the same period, they had encountered any difficulties in keeping up with regular payments, such as rent, hire purchase, or maintenance payments to a former partner. The second measure related to whether lack of money had prevented them from doing certain things which may have had an effect on their ability to look for jobs, for example: keeping up contacts with friends and relatives, keeping a vehicle on the road, dressing smartly for interviews, or arranging childcare whilst looking for a job.

Amongst women, there was a very clear relationship between type of 'non-claimant' status and financial circumstances, with a consistent pattern emerging across all the measures used. Working women and women who were *'non-claimant' due to ineligibility* for benefits were the least likely to have financial difficulties. In terms of having to borrow money and having difficulties keeping up with payments, other 'non-claimant' women and unemployed women were the worst off, followed closely by full-time students (Table 6.10).

When we looked at the limits imposed on women by lack of money, there was more variation, depending on the measure used. Working women and those ineligible for benefits still came out best, on all measures except difficulties in arranging childcare. Unemployed women and 'non-claimant' women from group 2 (not required to sign on or receiving benefits other than Income Support) were most likely to have been prevented from keeping up contacts with friends or relatives by lack of money. However, unemployed women and students (including women on government training schemes) were the most likely to say that money had prevented them from travelling to look for jobs, keeping a vehicle on the road, or dressing smartly for job interviews. The difference on these measures is likely to reflect variations in their relevance for women in different groups: for example, a woman who is truly inactive, in the sense that she does not intend looking for work is less likely to find that money has prevented her from travelling to look for jobs or dressing smartly for interviews, if she is not involved in either of these activities. Similarly, 'non-claimant' women were more likely to find that money prevented them from arranging childcare to look for work because a higher proportion of them had young children who required such care.

Among the men, the two groups most likely to have had to borrow money or to have had difficulty keeping up regular payments were the unemployed and *'non-claimant' men of indeterminate benefit status.* Working men were the least likely to have encountered financial difficulties in general. However, looking at the proportions of respondents who had needed to borrow money in the last six months, non-claimant men (*except* those from group three) were also less likely to have had to do so than non-working men from other groups.

Unemployed men were the most likely to have been prevented from keeping up contacts with friends or relatives, travelling to look for jobs, dressing smartly for job interviews and, together with students and men from the indeterminate 'non-claimant' group, from keeping a vehicle on the road. Students, including men on government training, and 'non-claimant' men from group three were the next most likely to have encountered difficulties with all of these things. The other two groups of 'non-claimant' men had fewer difficulties, and working men encountered the fewest difficulties. It is interesting to note that the difference we saw between women from 'non-claimant' groups one and two was not replicated among men. As we pointed out earlier, men who are ineligible for benefit (group one) are a less clearly defined group than women who are ineligible for benefit, most of whom had partners who were employed full-time. It is not surprising that fewer differences are observable between the two groups of men in terms of their financial circumstances.

It is also important to note that group two of 'non-claimant' men includes the substantial sub-group on sickness or invalidity based benefits, which is a smaller sub-group in the case of women.

The tables giving details of these comparisons are presented after the end of the chapter (Tables 6.10 - 6.13).

This brief review of financial and material circumstances does *not* support the view that any group of 'non-claimants' experiences on average more adverse conditions than those who are unemployed. Women moving into 'non-claimant' status by reason of ineligibility for benefits generally showed fewer signs of financial stress than unemployed people, presumably because they had husbands who were employed. Those moving onto income support based on lone parenthood, illness or disability would generally fare better financially than when on unemployment benefits. On the other hand, the review has brought to light a sub-group of 'non-claimant' people with indeterminate benefit status, amounting to about 2 per cent of the total sample at the time of the second survey interview, whose financial circumstances seem in some respects as adverse as unemployment. These need further study, as the source and nature of their problems remains unclear.

Summary of chapter

Movement off the unemployment register into a non-employment status is quantitatively important, but has been under-researched. In this chapter, we were primarily concerned to establish what was the influence of Restart upon this form of transition. Some commentators had assumed that one of the main effects of Restart was to terminate unemployment claims which were not valid, so as to reduce unemployment without a corresponding increase in employment.

Our findings showed that there was a significant effect of Restart on movements into 'non-claimant' status, but only during the early part of the study-period. This contrasts with the findings relating to movements into jobs, and into ET, where the Restart effect was cumulative and appeared fully only over a period of a year. So far as movement into 'non-claimant' status was concerned, over the whole year there was no Restart effect, and there was indeed some (inconclusive) evidence that Restart in the long term *delayed* movement into 'non-claimant' status.

The lack of a sustained Restart effect left us with the problem of explaining why this was so, contrary to previous expectations. We have argued that the chief explanation lies in the fact that such movements off the claimant register are already strongly controlled by other influences. The multivariate analyses showed clearly who were the people most likely to leave in this way: women, those with young children, those with limiting disabilities or illnesses, and older workers. We further showed how these characteristics combined to produce particular patterns of circumstances leading into 'non-claimant' status: women with working husbands losing their eligibility for benefits, others adopting child-care roles, and older men with disabilities or pensions moving into sickness benefit or early retirement.

These interpretations were strongly supported by the reasons which individuals themselves gave to explain leaving the register. But the investigation of people's reasons revealed one further group which was important in the first stage of the study period. Those were people who became 'non-claimants' while waiting to take up a job or a placement. These were often younger people, who moved into relatively short 'non-claimant' periods from jobs or training, rather than direct from unemployment. Under the ILO/OECD definitions, they would usually be classified as unemployed rather than inactive. Their reasons for not claiming benefit remain largely unexplained.

Finally, we examined (to a limited degree) the financial circumstances of those who moved into 'non-claimant' status. It has been argued by some commentators that movement of this kind may lead to personal hardship. Our evidence does not remove the possibility that this happens in some cases. But *on average*, those moving into 'non-claimant' status showed fewer signs of financial difficulty than those who were unemployed. Among the likely reasons for this were (a) that those moving into this status often had good recent work records, which may have increased their resources, (b) some were moving onto sickness or invalidity terms of income support, and (c) many had working spouses or (less often) pensions. The most financially disadvantaged sub-group was the one we knew least about: namely, those whose benefit position is indeterminate (according to our data).

Although this analysis has, we believe, added to knowledge of a little researched area, there is clearly far more to be done. One of the aspects which we would highlight for future consideration is evaluation of the economic costs of movements into 'non-claimant' status. These may prove to be quite serious, in view of (a) the high levels of prior employment of many of these individuals, and (b) the long-term nature of most moves into 'non-claimant' status – despite the technical difference between this and economic inactivity.

Table 6.10 Women's financial circumstances

	Group*						
	1	2	3	4	5	6	ALL
Percentage who in last 6 months:							
Needed to borrow money	14	28	21	14	24	27	19
Had difficulty in keeping up regular payments	19	31	31	15	23	26	21
BASE	(206)	(78)	(29)	(521)	(105)	(305)	(1245)

(Base: women who responded to the second survey interview)

Group 1: inactive, ineligible for IS and not known to be receiving another benefit

Group 2: inactive, not required to sign in order to receive IS, or known to be receiving another benefit

Group 3: inactive, benefit status not determined

Group 4: working

Group 5: full-time student on course or government scheme

Group 6: signing on the unemployment register

Table 6.11 Limits imposed on women by lack of money

	Group*						
	1	2	3	4	5	6	ALL
Percentage prevented by lack of money from:							
Keeping up contacts with friends or relatives	21	36	21	17	28	36	24
Travelling to look for jobs	9	18	24	10	25	36	18
Keeping a vehicle on the road	10	15	14	11	17	19	14
Dressing smartly for job interviews	18	23	28	14	35	39	23
Arranging childcare while looking for a job	17	15	10	5	3	5	8
BASE	(205)	(78)	(29)	(525)	(106)	(304)	(1247)

*   See Table 6.10 for key to groups

Table 6.12 Men's financial circumstances

	Group*						
	1	2	3	4	5	6	ALL
Percentage who, in last 6 months:							
Needed to borrow money	21	23	41	21	29	36	29
Had difficulty in keeping up regular payments	31	28	41	19	26	37	29
BASE	(52)	(180)	(37)	(789)	(288)	(1078)	(2423)

*   See Table 6.10 for key to groups

Table 6.13 Limits imposed on men by lack of money

			Group*				
	1	2	3	4	5	6	ALL
Percentage prevented by lack of money from:							
Keeping up contacts with friends or relatives	27	36	41	21	39	46	36
Travelling to look for jobs	27	20	41	17	39	52	36
Keeping a vehicle on the road	21	20	35	19	35	34	28
Dressing smartly for job interviews	23	24	32	18	41	48	35
BASE	(52)	(180)	(37)	(784)	(288)	(1078)	(2419)

(Base: men who responded to the second survey interview)

* See Table 6.10 for key to groups

7   Job Search and 'Flexibility'

One of the most important, but difficult, areas of research on unemployment is concerned with the process of seeking a job. It is particularly important, from both an individual and a policy viewpoint, once people have entered long-term unemployment (with six months or more of unemployment behind them). By then, under the labour market conditions which have prevailed in recent years, the average time to find a job will be quite substantial, and the disadvantages facing the individual may be cumulative. Getting out of this situation calls for considerable perseverance in seeking a job despite rejection. At the same time, the difficulties for the placement and support services in helping the individual are also likely to increase.

If job search declines or ceases, the implications for the individual are likely to be chronic long-term unemployment. That is serious enough, but there are other implications for the working of the wider labour market. Competition in that labour market cannot work effectively if many people in practice cease to compete, and without competition, there is reduced downward pressure on the level of wages. Wage levels that are divorced from the level of unemployment will tend to perpetuate a high level of unemployment and so contribute to a vicious circle.

The difficulty of understanding job search lies in its complexity. Among the factors which have to be considered, in a moderately realistic investigation, are the job search actions which people take over an extended period of time, the motives which lead them to search or not to search, the sources of information about jobs which are accessible to them, and the way they focus their attention and apply their criteria. Further, a matter of prime interest is how these various aspects of job search impinge upon outcomes, especially upon the chances of getting a job.

A widely used concept to structure such an investigation is that of 'flexibility'. The term is often used by economists, relatively narrowly, to describe how far individuals adjust their wage criteria in response to new information about the job market. But it is both reasonable and useful to apply it more widely, in a psychological sense. Flexibility can then be thought of as a disposition to be adaptable in order to reach a goal (in this case, the goal of finding a job). It thereby incorporates spatial and occupational mobility, and the use of varied sources of information or varied techniques of job search, alongside adaptability of wage criteria. In short, one can think of an individual's job search strategy, as a whole, being relatively flexible or inflexible.

In this chapter, we will not attempt to provide a comprehensive analysis of the job search information from the Restart Cohort Study. That information was, in fact, particularly rich and to do it full justice would require a report in its own right. Our aim is the more limited one of considering how far the Restart process influences job search and flexibility. In order to do this, however, we will need to describe some of the main features of job search and flexibility within this sample.

The importance of job search for outcomes
The first question to be considered is how much difference is made by more or less job search. Does additional job search, in fact, lead to better chances of employment? Does the Restart effect itself operate through increased job search?

It is by no means obvious that it is large amounts of job search, rather than (say) judicious or thoughtful job search, which makes the difference to an individual's success. It is worth establishing, therefore, what impact is made by the sheer quantity of search. In doing so, however, we ought to be aware that the quantity of search may itself be influenced by much the same factors as influence success. This is a point which the next section will consider.

The most direct indicator of the quantity of job search, and one which has been used in much previous research, is the number of job applications made. Job applications were defined in the survey questionnaire as including letters, telephone calls, and personal visits to employers' premises to inquire about jobs. The frequency of applications was reported by individuals for the previous four weeks, or for the most recent period of four weeks (within the past six months) in which they were looking for work. In the case of those with a current job, this could refer to a period before the current job, or to a period within the current job if they were looking for a change of job, as many were. The eight per cent of respondents to the first survey who said that they had not been looking for work at all in the past six months were not asked the question, but allocated a score of nought. The replies were grouped into five bands: 0, 1-4, 5-9, 10-19, and 20 or more applications. Table 7.1 shows how the sample was distributed at the first stage survey interview, with separate figures for those with, and without, current jobs.

Table 7.1   Frequency of job applications in a four-week period

	None	1-4	5-9	10-19	20+
Not in job	14	36	34	9	6
In job	29	27	28	7	9
All	18	34	33	9	7

Base: all interviewed at first survey (N=4807)

It may seem strange that those in a job made generally fewer applications than those without jobs, and especially that nearly one in three of those in jobs had made no application in the most recent four-week period in which they had been seeking work. But, as already noted, many in jobs were still seeking a different job. It is consistent with the economic theory of job search that those in a job should be much more selective about applications; and it is plausible that people in this situation should have been scanning job advertisements, or asking around their friends, without getting to the point of making an application.

This information about job applications, collected at the *first* survey interview, was used in multivariate analyses to assess job-related outcomes over the *whole* survey period. Accordingly these analyses are based on those who took part in *both* survey interviews. To strengthen the causal interpretation of the analyses, we excluded those who were already in a job at the first survey interview; this also eliminates the problem of incomparability of responses which is evident from Table 7.1. The analyses relate to the influence of job search activity before the first interview on job outcomes over the next six months. The number of individuals for the analyses was reduced to 2401.

First, we looked at the *change in the proportion of time in employment*, comparing employment after the claim to the prior employment record of 1985-87 (see Chapter 5 for further details of this approach). The multivariate analysis[1] used the usual set of explanatory variables, described in Chapter 1, along with four variables to represent the various levels of job applications.[2] A variable to represent the difference between the control group and the Restart groups was included in the usual way.

The analysis confirmed the importance of job search in increasing the proportion of time spent in employment. For job applications in the range from 1-19 per four weeks, there were improvements in the percentage of time spent in employment in the range of 5.5 to 7.7 points. (These improvements are estimated relative to making no applications whatever.) However, making a few (1-4) applications was not much inferior to making many (10-19) applications, in terms of employment outcomes. Further, those saying that they made very many applications (20 or more) were relatively unsuccessful and did not improve their employment chances significantly relative to those making no applications.[3]

A further interest in the analysis, for the purposes of this report, is whether the Restart effect alters when job search is brought into the analysis. A marked reduction of the Restart effect along with a strong effect of job search would suggest that Restart operated wholly or largely through stimulation of job search. No change in the Restart effect would suggest that it operated largely independently of job search. It was the latter interpretation which was supported. In fact, despite the added job search effects, the Restart effect estimated in this model was somewhat larger, and of somewhat higher statistical significance, than in the analyses reported in Chapter 5. Those in the Restart groups were estimated to do better than those in the control group, by about seven percentage points, in terms of their relative time in employment.[4] This finding, incidentally, tends to confirm that the effect of Restart upon time spent in jobs was significant, particularly in the second six months of the study period. The design of the present analysis confines the Restart effect on employment chiefly to that period of the study by excluding those in jobs at the first survey interview. The significant effects from this analysis are graphically summarised in Figure 7.1.

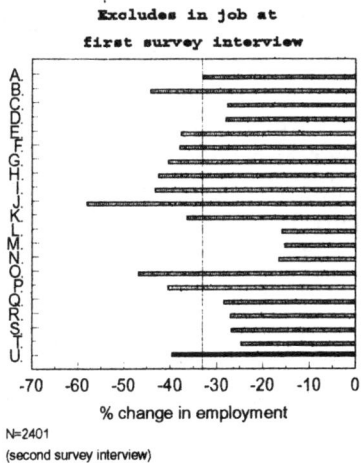

Fig. 7.1 Controlling for job search: Change in percentage of time spent in employment (post-Restart compared to 1985-87)

A. "Base case" respondent
B. Areas with highest labour turnover
C. Areas with lowest
D. Earliest start of claim
E. Latest start
F. Female
G. Aged 25-34
H. Aged 35-44
I. Aged 45-54
J. Aged 55 plus
K. Academic qualification
L. Divorced/widowed
M. Single
N. 1 child
O. 1 child under 5
P. Has driving licence
Q. Renting from council
R. 1-4 job applications
S. 5-9 job applications
T. 10-19 job applications
U. Control group member

Excludes in job at first survey interview

% change in employment
N=2401
(second survey interview)

The other employment outcome measure which we have used concerns the time taken to enter a job, from the starting point for the study. The technique of survival analysis, it should be recalled, not only assesses influence upon entry-time, but also takes properly into account the likely entry-times of those who had not entered a job by the end of the study period. (These were ignored in the preceding analysis.) The definition of the sub-sample, and of the explanatory variables, was exactly as in the preceding analysis.

Job search activity had, relative to the other explanatory variables, a still more powerful effect upon the time to enter a job than it had upon the proportion of time spent in employment. In this analysis, all four levels of job search had significant effects, and there was a marked increase in effect between making 1-4 applications (which reduced average time into employment by an estimated 40 per cent) and making 5-9 applications (which reduced time by an estimated two-thirds).[5] The apparently greater effect of job search upon entry time to jobs than upon the proportion of time spent in jobs can be interpreted along the lines developed in Chapter 5. Given a rather low level of stability in the jobs obtained, with many jobs ending quickly, a substantial part of the potential gain from early job entry is likely not to be realised.

Our chief interest in this analysis was again in the Restart effect. The statistical significance level of the Restart effect was lower than was found in Chapter 5, but the direction and estimated size of the effect were very similar to before. That is, the control group took longer on average to enter jobs than did the Restart groups.[6] The significant effects from this analysis are graphically summarised in Figure 7.2.

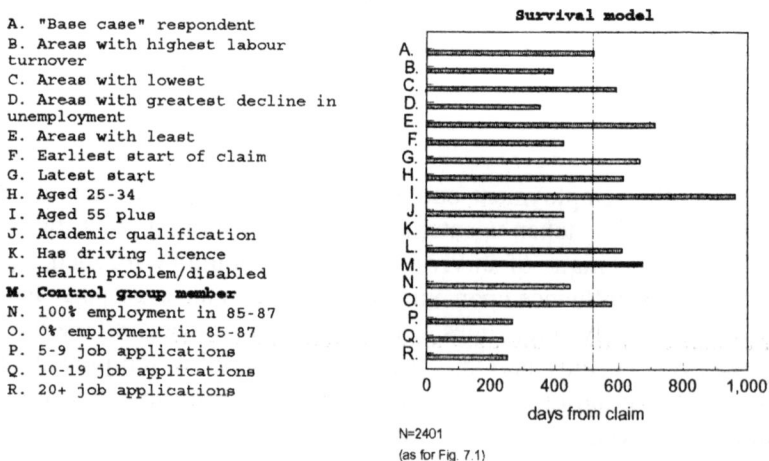

Fig. 7.2 Controlling for job search: Estimated time to enter employment

A. "Base case" respondent
B. Areas with highest labour turnover
C. Areas with lowest
D. Areas with greatest decline in unemployment
E. Areas with least
F. Earliest start of claim
G. Latest start
H. Aged 25-34
I. Aged 55 plus
J. Academic qualification
K. Has driving licence
L. Health problem/disabled
M. Control group member
N. 100% employment in 85-87
O. 0% employment in 85-87
P. 5-9 job applications
Q. 10-19 job applications
R. 20+ job applications

N=2401
(as for Fig. 7.1)

Taken together, the two analyses lead to three conclusions.

a) The quantity of job search, as measured by frequency of job applications, is important for employment outcomes, for people who are approaching one year of unemployment.

b) A moderate frequency of job applications, rather than an extremely high one, tends to bring the best overall returns.

c) The Restart effect appears to be independent of the quantity of job search.

Does Restart affect the frequency of job applications?

Although the evidence suggests that the Restart effect is independent of the quantity of job search, this is an inference which needs to be tested more directly. It would also be possible for Restart to have an influence upon job search in parallel with, or over and above, its influence upon employment outcomes.

An analysis was accordingly carried out, in which the variable to be explained or predicted was the frequency of job applications itself. The standard set of explanatory variables, including the difference between the control group and Restart groups, was deployed in the analysis. The analysis took account of the fact that the measure of job applications was not a true continuous scale, but a set of ordered categories.[7]

For this analysis, people responding to the first survey interview constituted the sample, *except that* those who were in a job at the time of that interview were excluded. Their exclusion was necessary in view of various preliminary analyses, which showed that levels of recent job search activity were not comparable between current job-holders and non-job-holders (see also Table 7.1 and associated discussion, above).

Rationality of search. One way of interpreting such an analysis, which has been put forward previously,[8] is in terms of the subjective rationality of the individual's job search strategy. If an individual is aware both of his or her own characteristics and circumstances, and of the effect these have on the probability of getting a job, then job search activity should also be affected by the same characteristics and circumstances. Assuming that the value of the outcome is a constant, then the lower the probability of achieving the outcome, the lower will be its expected value,[9] and the lower will be the search effort worth expending. Conversely, if individuals' levels of job search activity are influenced by more or less the same things as influence their objective chances of getting a job, then their job search strategies can be construed as, in a sense, rational. This formulation has been supported in previous research, but with a much more limited set of explanatory variables, and a more restrictive type of analysis, than was carried out here.

It should first of all be said that the analysis was, technically speaking, less successful than the majority of the multivariate analyses described in this report: it accounted for a relatively small proportion of the variation in job search activity. This suggests that some of the important influences upon job search were missing. Nevertheless, the results were generally clear and provided at least a provisional answer to the main questions of interest.

The analysis again found no significant relationship between participation in Restart and level of job search activity. Although the estimated effect was in the direction which would be expected on the assumption that there was a Restart effect (with the control group having less job search), this effect was statistically non-significant.[10] This non-significant result appears consistent with the findings from the previous section of this chapter, and with them suggests that the effect of Restart does not operate through individual job search.

The notion of search levels being chosen in proportion to expected chances of success got some support from this analysis, but it also seemed that some other factors might be present. The findings which accorded with expectations were that:

- Younger people searched more while older people searched less;

- those with qualifications, either educational or vocational, searched more;

- those with young children searched less;

- those with disabilities or illnesses searched less;

- those with much recent job experience searched more.

But other findings did not fit the 'rational choice' theory. The main discrepancies were that:

a) People in areas where the recent decline in unemployment had been relatively gradual (i.e., where jobs should be less available) engaged relatively more in search

b) People who had spent relatively large proportions of time as unemployed claimants in the past, were tending to engage in additional job search

c) People of Afro-Caribbean descent were engaging in more search than 'whites', while those of Asian descent were engaging in less.

Of these, factors (a) and (b) could be interpreted as compensatory efforts to make up for specific types of disadvantages, while factor (c) might be open to various speculative interpretations. In addition, women (who objectively had better chances of employment within this sample) engaged in much less job search. This agrees with much previous research, and seems to reflect a persistent difference of gender-related job markets, which has yet to be satisfactorily explained.

Restart 'actions' and job search activity

Although Restart as a whole could not be shown to stimulate job search activity, it remains possible that some of the paths within Restart might relate to it. In looking for such a relationship, however, one must be extremely cautious about causal types of inference. As we stressed earlier on, the various pathways within Restart represent processes of selection and self-selection, which are probably entangled with the outcomes which we are interested in.

Even in a purely descriptive sense, however, the following table (Table 7.2) reveals some striking contrasts between the levels of search activity among the Restart 'action' groups.

The danger of hasty causal inferences is illustrated by the case of the 'refused offer – referred for review' group. This emerges as having a particularly low level of job applications. But it is rather likely that the Restart counsellor's decision to refer the individual for review of entitlement to benefit would be influenced, in many cases, by the level of job search activity which was being demonstrated. If so, it would clearly be erroneous to attribute the low level of job search to the action taken in Restart. Similarly, the low level of job applications in the case of the 'excused interview' group cannot be attributed to the fact that members of this group had a reduced level of participation in the Restart process. Rather, it reflects the fact that this group contained the highest proportion of people getting jobs at an early stage of the study period, and the further fact that people with jobs were more selective about making further job applications.

Table 7.2 Job search activity levels by Restart 'actions'

	Low activity	Medium activity	High activity
Whole sample	17	67	16
'Placed'	13	67	20
'Submitted'	10	72	18
'Referred'	16	71	13
'Refused offer - not reviewed'	15	69	16
'Refused offer - reviewed'	38	53	9
'Offer not appropriate'	22	64	14
'Excused interview	37	49	14
'Failed to attend'	23	59	18

There was, however, one group within Restart for which an incidental influence of Restart upon job search activity might be claimed. This was the 'submitted, but not placed' group. The analysis which was presented in Chapter 3, concerning the characteristics of those in the various Restart 'action' groups, showed that the clients in this group tended to have one or more labour market disadvantages: low level of recent job experience, lack of a driving licence, responsibility for a young child. By the analysis of the previous section, these would also be expected to depress job search activity. Accordingly, there is no suggestion of selecting-in, in the sense of 'creaming off' on the basis of advantageous characteristics. We cannot exclude the possibility that apparent levels of job search influenced the original decision to put forward the individual for placement, but on balance it seems relatively unlikely. In that case, the apparently high level of job search in this group may have been influenced by Restart. The interpretation would be that a submission to a placement would tend to encourage the individual and increase levels of confidence; when the placement did not come off, the increased motivation would be re-directed into increased job search.

An analysis was conducted to test whether the apparently high level of job search activity in the 'submitted not placed' group was statistically reliable. For this analysis, we removed from the sample (a) those who were in a job at the time of the first survey interview, and (b) control group members, leaving 3,241 cases. Alongside the usual set of explanatory variables, an item was introduced to represent the difference between those in the 'submitted not placed' group and those in the other Restart 'actions'. Frequency of job applications was the outcome measure, as before.

The chief result of interest to our study was that the significance of the difference between the 'submitted not placed' group, and the average of the other groups within Restart, was confirmed. The effect was very highly significant.[11] Being submitted to a placement was linked to a substantially higher-than-average level of job applications.

From the viewpoint of interpretation, it is also important to check how much the effects of other variables within the analysis change when the 'submitted' effect is present. Substantial changes in the effects of any of the other variables would suggest that there is an overlap between that variable's effect and the 'submitted' effect. Absence of any such changes, on the other hand, would suggest that the 'submitted' effect is genuinely an additional one. In fact, there was little change in the estimated effects or significance levels of the other variables when the 'submitted' effect was introduced. This further increases the chances that the effect is a genuine one.

Because we excluded current job-holders from the analysis, it was desirable to test whether this affected the result. A sample selection model was therefore applied, and we were able to obtain a technically satisfactory solution.[12] In this more elaborate analysis, the effect of the 'submitted' group was virtually the same, and indeed there was little change in any of the significant influences upon job search activity. This indicates that the results are generalizable to the whole survey.

This analysis cannot be regarded as conclusive since, despite all contrary arguments, it is possible that submission to programmes or other forms of support are influenced by Restart counsellors' perceptions of the job search activities of the clients. The results do provide some evidence, however, to suggest that submitting people to programmes, even unsuccessfully, can stimulate job search, and these findings would be worth following up in future research which was focused more closely upon the counselling stage and could therefore address selectivity more directly. What can be said, with reasonable confidence, is that submitting people to programmes which they subsequently fail to enter does *not* adversely influence their job search.

'Dropping out' and Restart disciplines

It was noted earlier on that about eight per cent of the sample stated, at the first interview, that they had not been seeking work during the preceding six months (the time since Restart). This group can be considered to have 'dropped out' of the job market. By the time of the second interview, a further six months later, the corresponding figure had increased to 15 per cent. Since one of the aims of Restart is to ensure that individuals are making positive efforts to seek work, can this measure be used as a performance indicator for the Restart process?

The short answer is that it cannot. Why this is so is shown in Table 7.3, which breaks down the 'drop out' group into various components.

Table 7.3   Circumstances of those not looking for work in the preceding six months, at the first and second interviews

	First interview	Second interview
	per cent of total sample at interview	
All not seeking work	8.2	15.2
Of which:		
On Employment Training	1.1	2.7
Full-time education	0.3	1.1
Non-employed, non-claimant	4.5	8.8
Claiming as unemployed	2.3	2.6

It is the bottom row of this table which represents the best estimate of the proportion of claimants who were not seeking work for a long period, and this estimate points to a figure between two and three per cent. This figure should be reasonably reliable because of the particular care taken to establish the non-claimant, non-employed status in this survey.

The evidence of the survey, then, does not suggest that claiming while not seeking work was a substantial problem. It is not possible to state to what extent the Restart procedures had been responsible for this situation. At the second interview, while the proportion of 'claimant drop outs' among the Restart group was 2.4 per cent, it was 5.9 per cent in the control group. This might suggest a Restart effect but, because of the small sample size for the control group, not much reliance can be placed upon the result.

Flexibility

The survey questionnaires contained many items to explore various aspects of flexibility, both relating to wages and to other aspects of job search behaviour and attitudes. Our aim is to consider this section of information just sufficiently to establish its relevance to Restart.

Wage expectations. In Chapter 5 some simple descriptive information about wage outcomes was presented. It can be argued, however, that actual wage outcomes are rather a dubious measure of wage flexibility of individual job-seekers, since, apart from other considerations, they are determined at least as much by the policies and practices of employers as by the behaviour of job-seekers. From this viewpoint, more subjective measures of wage expectations may be preferable.

At both the first and the second interviews, questions were posed concerning the wages expected in a new job (which can also be regarded as individual targets), and also about willingness to settle for a lower figure (related to the economists' notion of a reservation wage). In interpreting this information, it is important to realise that past research has shown a low degree of correspondence between wage expectations or reservation wages, as stated by the individual, and the actual wages which people settle for when a real job comes on offer. This had led some researchers to abandon questions about wage expectations in favour of procedures to impute a reservation wage from (say) past employment.[13]

Notwithstanding this point, what people say about their wage expectations retains some interest in showing the way they approach their search for a job. It is also of interest to see whether participation in the Restart process affects wage expectations. The economic theory of job search[14] suggests that as a person's confidence in their own worth, or in the likelihood of getting a job, increases, so too should wage expectations rise and job search be stimulated by belief in better returns to the effort invested.

Table 7.4 shows the average expected wages reported by people at the first survey interview (excluding those not seeking work, or not providing complete information). The table also shows the hours of work which people expected to work for the money they had in mind. An hourly pay figure was calculated subsequently from this information.

Table 7.4 Wage expectations at the first survey interview

	Control group	Restart group
Average weekly wage	£ 115.9	117.9
Average hours	38.6	39.4
Average hourly wage*	£ 3.00	2.99
N (unweighted)	3662	195

Base: those seeking work, or in work, and providing full wages and hours information

* calculated from replies concerning weekly wages and hours

The slight indication of higher expected weekly wages among the Restart group, by comparison with the control group, was not statistically significant. In any case, once that the slight differences in expected weekly hours were taken into account, the expected hourly pay between the two groups was virtually identical. At the second stage interview (figures not shown), it was the expected weekly pay which was virtually identical between the groups (£123.50 for the controls, £124 for the Restart participants), while differences in the hours led to a rather larger apparent difference in hourly wage expectations (£3.33 against £3.20). Once again, though, none of these differences was statistically significant.

Are expected wages in any way related to job search activity? Theory would suggest that a higher reservation wage should be related to more job search, although this is based on 'other things being equal'. A very simple view of the present data offered some limited support, but the difference was found only between the lowest level of job search activity on one hand (no applications in a four-week period), and all higher levels of activity on the other. There was no systematic variation in pay expectations within the latter group. The group with low activity had average hourly pay expectations of £2.75, compared with £3.02 for the remainder, and this difference was statistically significant.

The average expected or target wages were higher than the actual average weekly wages, reported in Chapter 5, in the new jobs obtained by the time of the first survey interview. A large part of the difference, however, was accounted for by the new jobs being for shorter average hours than those assumed when individuals were stating their weekly pay targets. Most people assumed a full-time working week when presenting their wage targets, whereas a substantial number of the new jobs actually obtained were for part-time hours. In terms of weekly pay, the difference between target and actual was about £22, or nearly 25 per cent above the actual average wage, but in terms of hourly rates, the difference was only £0.26 or about nine per cent above the actual average hourly rate. A gap of nine per cent would easily be bridged by the difference between target wages and reservation (minimum acceptable) wages, which previous research has generally shown to be in the range of 15-30 per cent.[15]

Quite a substantial proportion of the present sample, however, stated that they would not be prepared to consider a lower wage than the target or expected wage that they had specified. The proportion unwilling to reduce their wage targets was 40 per cent (the question was not asked of those who had ceased looking for work for six months). But, as was mentioned earlier, this position would not necessarily be maintained in the face of an actual job offer. We did not pursue the relation between unwillingness to change the wage target and actual wages in jobs subsequently obtained, since with a small control group size, we could not have produced any reliable results with respect to Restart effects. Rather, we viewed unwillingness to reduce wage targets primarily as an attitudinal measure, and concentrated upon exploring its possible importance in relation to other aspects of flexibility and in relation to Restart.

In general, we found only small (and often non-significant) links between the willingness or unwillingness of individuals to consider a lower wage, and other aspects of job search and flexibility. Moreover, these relationships were not always as expected. For example, among those unwilling to lower their wage target, 50 per cent were seeking for a particular kind of job rather than being open to any job on offer, but this *rose* to 54 per cent in the case of those willing to lower their wage target. Similarly, among those unwilling to lower wages, 65 per cent wanted to use existing skills and experience in their new job, whereas this rose to 70 per cent among those willing to lower wages. A result more in accordance with conventional notions of flexibility was that 35 per cent of those unwilling to lower wages, but 43 per cent of those willing to lower wages, felt that they would move to a different area of the country if they had a job lined up there. Again, 16 per cent of those unwilling to lower wages, but 21 per cent of those willing to lower wages, came within the two highest frequencies of job applications.

Interpreting these results, it would seem that people are to some extent prepared to trade-off wages for the chance of getting a job which suits their interests and skills. This seems rational, as interests and skills are types of personal capital which individuals may do well to preserve. In some other respects, however, willingness to be flexible over wages was associated with other forms of flexibility in the job market, such as the willingness to search extensively.

Given this initial analysis, one might well have predicted that those participating in Restart would have a greater willingness to lower their wage targets. The findings, however, were if anything in the opposite direction. Of those in the control group, 34 per cent expressed unwillingness to reduce their wages, while the proportion in the case of those passing through Restart was 40 per cent. This difference was on the borderline of statistical significance. Restart did *not* lead to greater flexibility in terms of willingness to lower wage targets.

Restart and other kinds of flexibility. It was suggested earlier in the chapter that flexibility could usefully be viewed in wider terms than those of wages, and we have begun to do so already in the preceding paragraphs. In view of the rather negative findings from the analyses of wage flexibility and Restart, it seemed particularly necessary to consider whether there might be broader, perhaps more qualitative, forms of flexibility to which Restart might contribute.

To assess this, we first developed an 'index of flexibility' which was based on the following five aspects (three of which have already been referred to):

- willingness to consider taking part-time work
- willingness to consider taking short-term employment
- willingness to consider pay below the target level
- willingness to move to another area if a job was available
- whether the individual had actually visited a different area from his or her normal area of job search, in order to look for jobs.

These five items satisfied the chief condition for a composite index or scale, in that each item was positively associated with the other items and with the total 'score' for the scale. Individuals were scored 1 for each positive reply (zero otherwise), and these were summed to produce the index or total flexibility score. As none of these questions was asked of people who had withdrawn from job search, these were excluded from the analyses using this index.

Use of this scale failed to show any link between the Restart process and flexibility, even in a wider sense. The mean flexibility score for the control group was 2.20 while for the Restart group it was 2.27, a difference which was far from statistical significance. The more detailed distribution of scores is shown in Table 7.5 below, as this is of some intrinsic interest apart from the question of a Restart effect.

Table 7.5   Distribution of scores on the flexibility scale

column percentages

	Control group	Restart group
0:	3	6
1:	18	17
2:	32	31
3:	32	29
4:	11	15
5:	4	3

Base: those interviewed at the first survey interview and seeking work within the past six months.

The table shows that nearly one half of the sample was prepared to be flexible in three or more of the five ways considered in the scale. Eighty per cent were prepared to be flexible in two or more of the ways specified. The lack of a Restart effect here cannot be attributed to any technical failure of the questions, which spread out the sample in a satisfactory distribution.

Summary of chapter

The main aim of this chapter has been to assess how far the effects of Restart, identified in the previous chapters, might be interpreted as operating through processes of job search and through a willingness to be flexible or adaptable in the job market.

A preliminary step was to test whether, in fact, a high level of job search activity had a positive influence upon employment. Using the frequency of job applications as the representative measure, we showed that job search was highly important both for increasing the proportion of time in employment, and even more so for reducing the time taken to enter employment. But, in these analyses the Restart effect upon employment outcomes, described in Chapter 6, persisted with little alteration. This made it relatively unlikely that the Restart effect operated through influences upon job search, because if it had, then controlling for job search would have reduced the Restart effect.

A more direct approach, in which it was sought to explain levels of job search through Restart participation (along with other explanatory variables), did not produce a significant Restart effect. This again suggested that Restart did not operate through job search.

That conclusion, however, refers to Restart as a whole. Some part of the Restart process might still affect job search. A further analysis, therefore, looked specifically at whether being submitted to a placement through Restart was linked to an increased level of job search. The analysis showed that there was such a link. It is plausible, but far from certain, that this is a causal influence. Further research would be needed to confirm whether particular aspects of the Restart process, if not the Restart process as a whole, can stimulate job search. This research would have to collect more information about selection processes within Restart.

The chapter then turned to a consideration of various aspects of individual flexibility, in relation to Restart. These investigations reached almost uniformly negative conclusions about any link between Restart and flexibility, whether in terms of wage expectations, willingness to reduce wage targets, or more qualitative types of flexibility.

In short, Restart does not appear to operate to any great degree, if at all, through job search or through increased flexibility. This, from one point of view, makes the Restart effect more impressive: it appears to act *additionally* to what have widely been regarded as among the most important processes affecting employment chances. The same findings, however, exclude the most obvious explanation for the Restart effect and make the task of interpretation more difficult. This will be the task of the next, and concluding, chapter.

8 Discussion and Conclusions

The Restart Cohort Study aimed to provide answers to two questions: What difference did Restart make?, and, How did it achieve its effects? In this concluding chapter, we summarise the findings which bear upon these questions, but we do so in a broad way, without repeating the details which are to be found in the earlier chapters. We try to clarify those aspects of the questions which the study has been able to answer, and those which it has not been able to answer.

The research brief, to which this study was carried out, also spoke of the need for the study to contribute to the improvement of Restart or of similar schemes in the future. In attempting to make a contribution of this kind, the concluding discussion seeks to place Restart in a wider labour market context and to consider how systems could work better in cooperation. This, however, is a large theme and our views are tentative rather than assertive.

The research was confined to those approaching six months of a current unemployment claim. In speaking of Restart and its effects, it should be understood that we are not considering the application of Restart after longer periods of unemployment.

Restart has made a difference
The findings of this study consistently confirmed the view that Restart has made a difference at the individual level. During the study period (1989-90), those passing through Restart, compared with the control group, spent less time in claimant unemployment, made their initial movement off the register more rapidly, entered jobs more rapidly, spent more of their time in both jobs[1] and Employment Training, and, at the end of the study period, were more likely to be in employment and ET and less likely to be on the register. It also in the very short-term increased the time spent in a non-employed, non-claimant status,

although that effect disappeared or was reversed when the study period was considered as a whole.

A natural subsidiary question is how large these Restart effects have been. This is a question which can be answered in two main ways. One, likely to be of chief interest to those concerned with a cost-benefit type of assessment, is to look at the estimates supplied by the statistical analyses. The other, more useful to those who want to obtain a qualitative sense of Restart's impact among all the other influences in the labour market, is to consider how the Restart effect compares with other well-known influences upon outcomes in unemployment.

The statistical estimates, as so often, are less clear cut than one might have wished, even when the judgement that there is a significant effect is a reliable one. The central or 'best' estimates for the overall reduction of claiming within the study period, attributable to Restart, lie close to a figure of five per cent. It has to be remembered, however, that statistical estimates have margins of error associated with them. The true figure can only be assumed to lie, by the conventions applied by statisticians, somewhere between two and eight per cent. In addition, this estimate very probably understates the overall Restart effect, because it does not give any special weight to those who remained on the register at the end of the study period.

The comparative and qualitative assessment of the Restart effect seems a much surer one. The difference made by Restart was, in various analyses, of about the same order as (and sometimes greater than) the difference between being qualified or non-qualified, married or non-married, fit or in poor health, in a favourable or an unfavourable local labour market. The effect of Restart was only consistently exceeded by the effects of age and of gender. A five per cent difference made by Restart may not sound impressive, but it has to be set in a context where many factors have an influence upon outcomes, and no factor has a dominant influence. Relative to the modest size of many of the well-known influences upon unemployment, in these analyses, the size of the Restart effect seems almost worryingly large.

Genuineness of the Restart effect

Could the Restart effect, in reality, be an artificial result of the study design? A number of possibilities have to considered under this heading.

One concern is whether the composition of the control group could, in some way, have been contaminated. The selection of the controls, and the main sample, by means of National Insurance digits provided a powerful means of eliminating selection bias. But it is true that, in a real-life setting, a control group is less 'controlled' than in the laboratory. In particular, the ability of control group members to select themselves back into Restart, by asking for a Restart counselling interview, could have created a bias. But numerous tests were made and precautions taken in the analysis, in connection with this potential source of bias. We showed that, in terms of composition, job search behaviour, and attitudes, the control group was indistinguishable from the main sample. We also systematically tested for the presence of bias by using two different criteria for control group definition, which (if bias had been present) should have led to consistently different results. But we got similar results from both types of analysis.

Another potential problem concerns the effect of non-response, a perennial anxiety with surveys. In this case, however, we had exceptional scope for analysis, based on administrative records, of non-respondents as well as respondents, and exceptional chances of checking the effects of non-response directly. The outcomes for non-respondents were substantially better than for respondents, but the important point is that this difference did not 'bend' the Restart effect to an appreciable degree, in either direction.

An important question is how far the findings of a study relating to individuals can lead to conclusions about the aggregate labour market. It may be argued that the differences in outcomes between the control group and the Restart groups are real, but that they are only applicable to the situation where Restart is the normal process. In other words, according to this argument, the difference between the control group and Restart participants is not the same as the effect if nobody took part in Restart. When everybody goes through Restart, there is a competitive disadvantage in not going through it; but if nobody went through Restart, everyone would be on the same level. The differential effect cannot be equated with the aggregate effect.

One approach to assessing the relevance of the present findings at the aggregate level is to set it within a more theoretical view of labour market processes. Our interpretation of the chief findings of this study (which will be developed in further detail below) is that Restart links unemployed people more efficiently into various resources for getting themselves out of unemployment, and also provides a 'time discipline' both for individuals and for services. This is, essentially, an interpretation in terms of supply-side improvement of the labour market. It may also be developed further, depending upon one's theoretical predelictions, in terms of increased labour market competitiveness leading to a variety of salutary longer-term adjustments in the labour market. If aggregate outcomes are responsive to the supply side, then equipping people with additional competitive resources should produce an aggregate improvement. Conversely, to suppose that such supply-side changes have no aggregate effects appears to require that outcomes are largely or wholly determined from the demand side of the labour market.

In this connection, a conclusion reached in a recent major review of unemployment by Richard Layard, Stephen Nickell and Richard Jackman is worth quoting in full:

> Discussions of displacement normally involve a profound misconception. They assume that demand is limited, so that if someone gets a job there is one less job for others... However,.. demand can easily be changed. What puts a limit on feasible demand is feasible supply... in the long run, the supply side rules.[2]

This view goes somewhat further than the present authors would. In our view, the aggregate behaviour of the labour market depends on all its actors, both those on the demand side and those on the supply side. There seems to us, however, no good theoretical grounds whatever for assuming that changes on the supply side have no aggregate effect.

There is, however, little point in theoretical debate if an issue can be tackled by research and measurement. There have in fact been two macroeconometric studies which have estimated the aggregate effects of Restart. Although these studies used very different modelling methods, they each concluded that there was a substantial aggregate effect of Restart; indeed, they have each attributed to Restart a major, perhaps the major, influence on reducing unemployment during the boom period of the late 1980s.[3]

In our view, the assessment of major labour market developments can rarely be carried out or demonstrated through a single definitive study. Research is a cumulative process in which various studies, applying different methods, have to be brought to bear. The fact that the present study, at the individual level and using a cross-sectional sample, is in broad agreement with independent studies at the macro level and using time-series analyses, helps to strengthen confidence in the genuineness of the effects of Restart.

Generality and limitations of the Restart findings
Another question which needs to be directed at the findings concerns their generality. How far do they simply reflect a particular sample, a particular time, a particular set of labour market conditions?

The study was exceptional in the fact that it was based upon a completely unclustered national sample. Spatially, it was unusually representative and its findings should have a higher degree of generality to Great Britain than most sample surveys. The survey was also of large size, and, being drawn over a period of four months, was unlikely to be affected by very short-term conditions.

The most obvious limitation of the survey was that it was confined to the inflow at six months of unemployment, whereas Restart interviews are given to people at six monthly intervals throughout unemployment. The Restart interviews directly considered by the study relate to perhaps 30 per cent of all the Restart interviews which take place annually. It is not possible to generalise the Restart effect found in the present study to all Restart interviews. On the other hand, the Restart effect identified in the present study does apply to all Restart *participants*, because everyone who is involved in the Restart process at later stages of unemployment will also have passed through the initial Restart process at six months. The effect identified here can therefore be thought of as a *lower bound* estimate of the total *per individual* Restart effect.[4]

The other chief limitation of the Restart Cohort Study is that it took place under the specific labour market conditions of 1989 and the first half of 1990. During 1989 the labour market was buoyant; during 1990 it was beginning to go into a recession, although this was not apparent until some way into the year. Moreover, at the time when the sample was being drawn, in late 1988, there had already been the best part of a year of buoyant labour market conditions, so that the people reaching six months of unemployment at that time might be rather different from those reaching the same point in late 1991, after a year of rising unemployment.

The particular argument which could be put forward is that Restart is more likely to be effective in a buoyant labour market, which is tending towards supply-side bottlenecks, than in a recessionary labour market which is facing lack of effective demand. In the former situation, the problem is to help people to get aboard plentiful opportunities, and this may be what Restart does best.

On the other hand, one could argue that the potential advantage of a systematic review and counselling process such as Restart is precisely that it is not tied to particular conditions. As a gateway or bridge to the various actions and programmes provided by the labour market services, it can operate with any mix of such actions and programmes. As labour market conditions change, naturally different actions and programmes are likely to be brought into play, but Restart can still help to provide the linkages or gateways. But, of course, this is to say that the effectiveness of Restart will depend to a considerable extent upon the programmes and services to which it can relate: a point to which we will return later. It is also true that different conditions, and different programmes to meet them, may call for different criteria to be applied when carrying out an evaluation study.

In short, it is correct to say that the present study does not demonstrate that a Restart effect of the same order would occur under different labour market conditions. But neither is there anything in the present study's findings which rules out the possibility of a continuing effect provided that there is appropriate adaptation to new circumstances.

As the final point under this section, it is worth noting that the present study began about three years after Restart was established as a national system. It may have missed any 'once-only' effects resulting from the inception of a systematic review process. Possibly, the longer a system remains in being, the more difficult it becomes to detect its effect, because they have become built into the assumptions and normal behaviour of the labour market.

How Restart works

The second aim of the study has been to improve understanding of how Restart achieves its effects. The picture which we wish to give is one of a wide range of smaller effects which accumulate to produce the overall Restart effect. The nature of the Restart process is to act as a link with many possibilities, to facilitate a variety of actions, and to impose a time-related review on the perhaps rather diffuse events as people enter long-term unemployment. The other chief characteristic which we see in Restart is to respond to individual difficulties or disadvantages and to seek some degree of remedial action.

This is necessarily a somewhat low-key, though wide-ranging, interpretation of Restart. To become convinced of its plausibility, it is useful first to rid oneself of simpler, bolder, monocausal views of Restart. Accordingly, we start by saying how Restart does *not* work.

Restart does *not* work primarily through a deterrent effect, operating against ineligible claims to benefit. There was, undoubtedly, some effect in increasing movements off the register and into non-claimant status, but it was not large, and it was present only in the first six months of the study period: by the end of the study period, the effect had vanished. Further, there was no indication of a specifically *early* effect of Restart, such as would have been visible if many people, knowing themselves to have ineligible claims, had been evading discovery at the Restart counselling interview.

Restart does *not* work solely as a link with Employment Training. Increased participation in ET was an important and significant outcome from Restart, but it was surprising how gradually the effect appeared and, at the end of the study period, how modest it was. The explanation for this must lie in the openness of access to ET, which results in less disadvantage for non-participants in Restart than might be imagined.

Restart does *not* gain an advantage by stimulating higher levels of job search or by creating a more flexible outlook towards job search on the part of unemployed people. Our analysis showed that job search was, indeed, highly important, but also that Restart, as a whole, was not systematically related to it. Regarding flexibility, our analyses were sufficient to show that Restart participation was little if at all related to it.

As a second step to understanding how Restart works, consider the main points which the study reveals about the *time-course* of its effects. We demonstrated that a substantial gap between the Restart group and the control group first appeared in the month after the Restart counselling interview. This would be the period when a basic review of the individual's position took place, and when links were established with a variety of programmes and services. At the other end of the study period, we also demonstrated that a substantially smaller proportion of the Restart group, than of the control group, remained continuously in unemployment or continuously without a job. There was therefore an overall Restart effect both one month after the counselling interview and twelve months after the counselling interview. Over that period, however, the components of the Restart effect were changing. Movement into 'non-claimant' status emerged earliest, but had died away by about six months after the counselling interview. Meanwhile, however, movement into ET and employment was increasing gradually, and these had emerged as significant during the second six months.

This picture of how Restart developed over the study period was to some extent rather unexpected. We expected to find most of the effect concentrated in the first six months, with a dying away in the next six as the control group members got the same access to programmes and services as the initial Restart participants. The pattern observed may indicate one or both of two things. It could be that the average time-lags are quite considerable between a person being directed towards a Jobclub, an ET assessment, an interview with the Disablement Resettlement service, or whatever, and the conversion of that into a job or an ET placement. It could also be that, by six months of unemployment, there are considerable difficulties on the side of many clients in responding to offers made, and that effects from Restart only begin to show as the difficulties are progressively overcome.

The difficulties or disadvantages faced by Restart's clients, and how Restart responds to these, provide another focus for our study. In Chapter 2 we already pointed out that some of the main characteristics of the sample could be seen in terms of disadvantage. Later chapters showed, with a variety of different approaches, that Restart generally operated in ways that favoured those with disadvantages. Sometimes this was direct and explicit, as in the referrals to the specialised services for disabled workers. But it also took the form of a more general tendency to submit those with relatively unfavourable prior employment records to the main opportunities on offer, such as Employment Training. Further, there was a small, but clear, tendency for those with disadvantages of various kinds to be more aware and appreciative of the support provided by and through Restart, than were others with better chances in the job market.

We can now try to put together these varied insights into how Restart worked. The resulting picture is, of course, to be seen very much as an interpretation rather than as a statement of fact.

First of all, Restart works by imposing a time discipline. This discipline applies in the first place to those entering long-term unemployment. The individual is required to take part in a review of his or her position at a set time. This review is likely to have several consequences. Those undecided about staying in the labour market or withdrawing from it (for example, because of ill-health or childcare considerations) may be brought to a decision. Others, thinking of taking various steps (such as applying for a place on Employment Training), may be encouraged to do so more rapidly than would otherwise have happened. Some, who are not seeking work, are placed in a position where their interests are tested and their benefit claim submitted to review. Restart may also constitute a time discipline for the programmes with which it has links. Not only does it submit individuals to these programmes, but it has a reporting system which requires that the outcome of those submissions should be followed up and recorded.

These elements of the time discipline indicate why a clear Restart effect emerges within about one month of the date of the counselling interview. Although at this early stage movement into non-claimant status is the main component of the Restart effect, some contribution from Employment Training and perhaps also from jobs may be present, although not detectable as significant separate effects.

Restart's effects, however, are not limited to the time discipline or to the impact of the counselling interview. The existence of further movements into jobs and Employment Training, during the period from six to 12 months after the counselling interview, suggest the existence of more diffuse and cumulative effects. Unlike the time discipline, these are not general effects applying across all who pass through Restart. They depend upon the particular actions which Restart gives rise to and the courses of events which result. Because these different routes through Restart imply the existence of selectivity and choice, cause and effect are hard to discern in any rigorous sense. But we know that clients with disadvantages are, on average, offered more opportunities through Restart. They are typically not offered one path, but a variety of paths. Nearly one in five come back for a second Restart interview. People have some scope, then, for exploring alternatives and making choices. All this would take time. Understanding these complications makes it less puzzling why some of the main Restart effects did not appear until the second half of the study period.

It needs to be stressed that what may not be true of Restart participants as a whole, may yet be true of sub-groups within Restart. For example, there was no overall Restart effect upon job search in this study, but there was an apparent positive effect upon job search for those people who were submitted to a placement through Restart, but did not enter it. Because there was no information about prior levels of job search, we cannot be sure that it was Restart which produced this difference. But it is a plausible interpretation.

More generally, we suggest that the discussion of a variety of potential opportunities, the support offered by counsellors in putting individuals forward and making initial appointments for them, and any subsequent actions taken by individuals to follow up these possibilities, should help to raise levels of activity in the labour market. All such effects, of course, are constrained in what they can achieve by the competitive position of individuals in the labour market, and by the way in which the wider labour market operates. Any one path through and beyond Restart is likely to have such small effects as to be undetectable against this background. But it is the totality of such effects which produces the overall Restart effect. So, as we have already said, the Restart effect depends in part upon the other possibilities with which it can connect people.

Limitations and further potential of Restart

A complete assessment should take account, not only of what has been achieved and the methods of achieving that, but also of what has not been achieved, what more might be achieved, and what are the constraints upon further progress. The capacity of a survey analyst for contributing to this wider type of assessment, however, is limited by the data available. Surveys consider a given situation; although it may be possible to point to current limitations which emerge from the analysis, it is usually difficult to offer practical suggestions for overcoming those limitations, which would need wider knowledge of the factors bearing upon policy and operational practice.

The most obvious way of approaching this type of assessment is by considering outcome measures where Restart participants did not fare better than control group members.

It should first be noted that no obviously *adverse* effects of Restart were identified by this study. For example, it might have been surmised that, by stimulating entry to Employment Training, Restart would have had a *negative* effect upon time spent in employment during the first part of the study. But this was not the case. Again, some commentators have suggested that Restart operates chiefly by forcing individuals off the claimant register into economic inactivity, where they may suffer substantial hardship because of unexpected loss of benefit entitlement. But we were unable to find evidence that those who withdrew into non-claimant status for reasons connected with benefits were, on average, in hardship of this kind. Although individual cases of this type may have existed, on average the group withdrawing for reasons of benefit entitlement seemed to be better off than those who continued on the register (who were consistently the group worst off). Similarly, some commentators had expressed the view that Restart, in conjunction with the 1989 Social Security Act, would force many people to take jobs at unusually low wages. Although our ability to analyse this aspect was limited by small sample size, so far as we could go we could see no difference between the wages in new jobs of Restart participants and of control group members.

The wage obtained is just one aspect, although an important one, of the wider concept of 'job quality'. Other aspects which we considered were occupational level and job stability. There were no indications that Restart was leading people, on average, to seek and obtain jobs at either lower or higher occupational levels, either relative to those not participating in Restart, or to their own previous occupational levels.

The other indicator of job quality – stability, or instability – seemed to constitute the clearest problem or limitation for Restart. As before, there was no clear indication that Restart participants were any worse off on this measure than non-participants, although small sample size in the case of the control group made comparison difficult. The chief practical point was simply that many of the new jobs obtained, for the sample as a whole, were in fact short-lived. Lack of stability in new jobs inevitably reduces the cost-effectiveness of a system like Restart.

This consideration of job quality illustrates one of the points which has been referred to several times already: Restart's potential depends partly upon the other programmes and services to which it is linked.

If these are not geared to raising aspects of job quality, then it is unlikely that Restart will do so. How job quality objectives might be built into programmes and services is an issue which falls outside our remit, but it is one which could repay some attention. An obvious objection is that any emphasis upon quality aspects might be to the detriment of the quantity of jobs on offer, surely the prime objective. It may be worth noting, however, that at the time of the 1988-89 jobs boom, many large employers were beginning a serious review of their internal policies in order to focus more upon retention and less upon recruitment.[5] This might provide an area of opportunity during the recovery from the present recession, when the theme of retention, with its obvious implications for job quality, is likely to re-emerge.

An area where the impact of Restart was perhaps disappointingly neutral was job search. Although there was no overall effect on job search, however, there were some indications that processes of submission to placements might, in an incidental fashion, stimulate greater job search. Unlike most other aspects of Restart, where the aim is to guide individuals towards other programmes, services or opportunities, in the case of job search the counsellor has scope for making an impact without the involvement of intermediaries. The lack of any systematic Restart effect in this area raises questions about how well equipped counselling staff (currently, Claimant Advisers) are for carrying out this role. In view of the strong impact of job search on labour market outcomes, further review of this aspect of Restart might prove worthwhile.

Another way of reviewing limitations is by considering whether any groups appear to participate to a lesser extent in the Restart process. Such groups could then be considered as opportunities for extending the effectiveness of Restart.

It might be thought that there is little scope in this direction, because Restart (in practice) already leans towards helping those with labour market disadvantages. But there are two groups where the evidence of this study suggests a possible need for further review. Both these groups are large ones.

In Chapter 3, we showed that *women* were on average offered access to fewer opportunities through Restart than were men, and that there was no opportunity in which women had advantageous access over men. This could well be a reflection of the programmes which Restart serves, notably Employment Training, where as is well known there have been three places for men for each place for women. But this is to some extent at least a chicken-and-egg argument: should one not ask, to what extent is the placement ratio in ET a reflection of the submission practice in Restart? The issue, in any case, is not limited to the offer of opportunities. We also showed that women were far more likely than men to be referred for review of their claim, after refusing an offer, even when we controlled statistically for marital status and the presence of young children in the family.

These points, however, would on their own give a one-sided view of Restart in relation to women. In the first place, women had if anything more favourable views of Restart than did men. More fundamentally, we tested statistically for the possibility that the Restart effect was different in the case of men than in the case of women. As far as we were able to go, we found no evidence for this. In other words, the difference in outcomes between women in Restart and women in the control group was similar to the difference between men in Restart and men in the control group. But this was one of the points where the analysis was limited by the size of the control group; for example, we would have liked to look at job-related Restart effects at the second-stage survey interview, as between men and women, but shrinking control group size made this difficult. The conclusion of 'no gender effect' is the best available one at present, but it should be drawn with caution.

The other group for which relatively limited options seemed to be available was older workers. As in the case of women, we tested whether the Restart effect took different values by age group, and found that it did not. Older workers passing through Restart got as much advantage over older workers in the control group as was the case for younger workers in Restart compared with younger workers in the control group. The scope for analysis by age group, however, was as limited as the analysis by gender which we have just discussed. So the conclusion of 'no age effect' should also be treated with caution.

It is, of course, much easier to point to a lack of opportunities for particular groups in unemployment than to offer proposals for how more opportunities could be provided. We would again like to point out, however, the potential significance of the new thinking which was emerging among some employers during the 1988-89 jobs boom. For the first time in many years, such employers were beginning to think in terms of special recruitment strategies for older workers and for women returners. This thinking could create new opportunities which might be exploited more fully at the time of the economic recovery.

Concluding comments on the implications of the study

The evaluation carried out through the Restart Cohort Study has led us to conclusions which are relatively straightforward.

First, we conclude that Restart, at the time of the study, was having effects at the individual level, of practical significance, upon reducing time as a claimant, and increasing time in Employment Training and in employment. It led to marked reductions in the initial exit-time from unemployment and in the initial entry-time to jobs and to ET or other programmes. These conclusions apply to the individual level, but are consistent with the findings of macroeconomic studies applying at the aggregate level.

Second, we conclude that Restart achieved its effects through a combination of smaller impacts spread over the year through which the study was carried out. These intermediate impacts reflected a wide range of actions applied, and opportunities offered, to different sub-groups on a selective basis. This method of achieving results was a natural consequence of the nature of Restart as a time discipline and as a gateway to the full range of programmes and services for the labour market.

Third, we conclude that Restart operated in a way which was particularly helpful to people with competitive disadvantages in the labour market.

We have however pointed to a number of areas to which further consideration could be given, in order possibly to increase the positive effects or helpfulness of Restart. We particularly drew attention to the potential contribution to cost-effectiveness which would arise through increases in the stability of jobs into which people move, and of developing more effective guidance on job search. There might also be scope for improving the balance of opportunities towards women and towards older workers. All these are areas where the scope for improved policies might be explored in consultation with employers and with Training and Enterprise Councils. We stressed, however, that improvements in these respects could not be expected (with the possible exception of guidance on job search) simply through developments within Restart itself. Restart might however contribute in conjunction with developments in the wider labour market systems and programmes.

Although numerous further implications might be drawn from the results, we will confine ourselves to two, which appear to be of a particularly high order of importance.

The first concerns the implications of the research method used in this study. Most unusually for the UK, a control group design was introduced. The experience of working with such a design has shown how much better the questions of interest to an evaluation study can be answered through control group comparisons than without. The control group was small, and this imposed some limitations upon what could be achieved in the analysis. Nevertheless, the conclusions of this research simply could not have been reached without the control group. Further, a larger control group would have permitted the total cost of the study to be reduced at the same time as extending the scope for analysis considerably, especially in regard to wages outcomes.

This practical experience is in accordance with a recent review of evaluation research published by the OECD.[6] The superiority of control group designs over the more usual comparison group studies is strongly affirmed by this review.

It is suggested that the further scope for use of control group designs in the evaluation of government programmes, and the cost-benefit implications, could usefully be reviewed on the basis of the experience of the present study.

The second, and most important, implication of the present study concerns the potential effectiveness of active labour market policies, or more generally, for supply-side stimulation of the labour market. In the past two decades, the consensus among labour market specialists has moved progressively towards belief in the importance of the supply side and of active policies for increasing labour market flows. As described in Chapter 2, the persistence of unemployment during much of the 1980s gave rise to new qualitative constraints on the supply side which, it was argued, needed to be directly addressed by active labour market policies. It is, however, difficult to provide practical demonstrations of the supposed effects of such policies.

Restart is an excellent example of a 'pure' supply-side policy. It acts as a gateway into the labour market programmes and services and helps to facilitate the flows into and between them. Nor can it be said to be a particularly intensive or costly intervention on the supply side, since the average total cost per interview has been of the order of £20-25.[7]

The evidence from this study of a substantial effect from the Restart process, taken in conjunction with other studies applying different perspectives and methods, offers support for the view that active policies on the supply side can improve labour market outcomes. We would not of course wish to argue that this makes the demand side irrelevant or even any less important. We hope, however, that this study will further stimulate interest in the potential of active supply side policies for contributing to reductions in unemployment.

Notes and References

Chapter 1

1. The 1980-82 Cohort Study of the Unemployed Flow sponsored by the (then) Manpower Services Commission was of similar size and considered a sample of about 8,000 people of all types entering unemployment. By about five-six months after the initial sampling date, the number remaining in unemployment was reduced to about 4,000. See Daniel, W.W. *The Unemployed Flow*, Policy Studies Institute, 1990, for further details. Other studies of unemployed people during the 1980s used smaller samples or excluded larger sections of unemployment. For example, the 1983-84 study of living standards in unemployment sponsored by the Department of Social Security consisted of 2,925 interviews and was confined to unemployed heads of households.

2. The absence of clustering is statistically advantageous. When a clustered design is used, the standard errors of statistical estimates are affected and it is often difficult to allow for this in a rigorous way.

3. Some of the cases excluded may have arisen because of differences in definition of claim period between the Restart procedure and the JUVOS system of unemployment statistics. The JUVOS system links together successive claims by an individual which are separated by a very short gap, treating them as one continuous claim. In that case, their inclusion in the Restart Cohort sample would not be incorrect from the point of view of the sampling procedures laid down for this study. However, we had no means of checking the nature of such discrepancies. We decided to exclude all of them since this would reduce heterogeneity in the sample and minimise the presence of errors. The exclusions applied equally to the Restart group and to the control group.

4. The control group members noted on the administrative procedures as receiving a Restart interview amounted to about one half of those reporting that they had had a Restart interview. The administrative information does not make it fully clear whether the interview took place because of a request from the individual or not. Where an individual reported a Restart interview but it was not noted on the administrative records, this could reflect either misremembering on the part of the person, or a late interview which was missed by the recording process, or an administrative slip in failing to record the interview.

5. See: LaLonde, R.J. 'Evaluating the Econometric Evaluations of Training Programs with Experimental Data', *American Economic Review*, vol.76, 1986; Riddell, C. 'Evaluation of Manpower and Training Programmes: the North American Experience', in Organisation for Economic Co-operation and Development, *Evaluating Labour Market and Social Programmes: The State of a Complex Art*, OECD, 1991.

6. If people moving from the control group into Restart are self-selected by characteristics which positively affect their chances in the job market (e.g. strong motivation), then removing them from the control group will lead to an overestimate of the Restart effect. If on the other hand they are self-selected by reason of attributes negatively related to their chances in the job market (e.g. they are relatively 'dependent' or in need of support), then removing them from the control group will lead to an under-estimate of the Restart effect. Further, the mode of entry to Restart from the control group might be different from the 'regular' mode of entry and this might also affect outcomes. For example, people from the control group might be expected to move into Restart relatively late, could delay other job market activity while awaiting a Restart interview, and might have missed out on opportunities available to those entering Restart 'on time'. In that case, retaining the Restart participants in the control group will lead to an over-estimate of the Restart effect. Conversely, if having a 'non-standard' Restart interview is advantageous (this is harder to visualise), then retaining Restart participants in the control group will lead to an under-estimate of the Restart effect. (For evidence of the disadvantaging nature of 'non-standard' entry to programmes, see: Greaves, K. *The Youth Opportunities*

Programme in Contrasting Local Areas, Manpower Services Commission, Research and Development Series No. 16, 1983; White, M. and McRae, S. *Young Adults and Long-term Unemployment*, PSI, 1989, Chapter 5.)

Finally, random movement into Restart from the control group might result from simple administrative error, or from chance contacts between claimants and Jobcentre staff which brought Restart interviews to mind. In this case, it would not affect the accuracy of the estimates of the Restart effect whether the Restart participants were included or excluded from the control group.

7. Strictly speaking one should control for other characteristics, such as age, gender, etc., while assessing the association between control group membership and an attitude. However, as we have already shown that there was no relationship between control group membership and the set of characteristics which we normally apply, this complication in the analysis was superfluous.

8. The two associations were significant only at the five per cent level, despite the large sample size for these analyses (N=4,807). The differences identified were only of the order of 3-5 per cent in a cell proportion between control group and Restart group members. There was no clear pattern to the results. Such associations as apparently identified, therefore, would most reasonably be attributed to chance (note that, if 20 tables are analysed, then one 'significant' result at the five per cent level will be expected on a purely chance basis).

9. Disney, R. and others, *Helping the Unemployed: Active labour market policies in Britain and Germany*, Anglo-German Foundation, 1992.

10. It should be noted, however, that economic theories of job search tend to derive a positive relationship between reservation wage level and the amount of job search. So, if Restart were to reduce reservation wage levels, it could also reduce the effective level of job search; hence the net effect on aggregate wages would be indeterminate.

11. We begin with a relatively small control group, and this is further reduced since only a minority gets a job during the survey period. Additional losses of data arise because one in five of the sample

had no previous job (hence no previous wage against which comparisons might be made), and there were fairly substantial gaps in the current wage or hours of work data of those in jobs, because of self-employment, short period in job, variable hours or payment, etc. At the time of the first survey interview, for example, we had complete wage and hours data on only 46 control group members, and this was clearly inadequate for multivariate analysis.

12. For introduction to survival analysis, see: Allison, P.D. *Event History Analysis: Regression for Longitudinal Event Data*, Sage Publications, 1984.

13. Breen, R. *Education, Employment and Training in the Youth Labour Market*, The Economic and Social Research Institute (Dublin), Central Research Series No. 152, 1991.

14. Censored regression analysis is also commonly referred to as Tobit analysis. For an explanation, see Green, W.H. *Econometric Analysis*, Macmillan, 1990; or Maddala, G. *Limited-Dependent and Qualitative Variables in Econometrics*, Cambridge University Press, 1983. In non-technical terms, what Tobit analysis does is to bring together information about the cases at the limiting value and information about the cases in the continuously varying part of the distribution. The resulting analysis must always be more efficient than consideration of either type of information on its own.

15. For further explanation, see Green, *op. cit.*; Maddala, *op. cit.*

16. See LaLonde, *op. cit.*

17. See Green, *op. cit.*, for remarks on the inefficiency of the widely used Heckman method.

18. The difficulty arises because of the special problems created by unobserved variables in longitudinal data. For explanation, see Lancaster, A. and Nickell, S. 'The Analysis of Reemployment Probabilities for the Unemployed', *Journal of the Royal Statistical Society*, Series A, vol.143, 1980; Heckman, J.B. and Borjas, G.J. 'Does unemployment cause future unemployment?' *Econometrica*, vol.47, 1980.

19. The exponential distribution can be considered as a special case of the Weibull distribution, in which the time parameter equals one.

20. The Weibull distribution involves introduction of an additional free parameter into the model. The value of this can be assessed by comparing the log-likelihoods of the Weibull and exponential models on one degree of freedom.

Chapter 2

1. See: Barro, R. 'The persistence of unemployment', *American Economic Review*, vol.78, 1988; Organisation for Economic Cooperation and Development, *Economies in Transition: Structural Adjustment in OECD Countries*, OECD, 1989.

2. Hughes, P. 'Flows on and off the unemployment register', *Employment Gazette*, December 1982.

3. For such reviews, see: Lindbeck, A. and Snower, D. 'Explanations of unemployment', *Oxford Review of Economic Policy*, vol.1, 1985; Holmlund, B. *Unemployment Persistence and Insider-Outsider Forces in Wage Determination*, OECD Working Papers No.92, February 1991.

4. Our comments on hysteresis are at a non-technical and non-rigorous level. For further explanation see: Cross, R. (ed.), *Unemployment, Hysteresis and the Natural Rate Hypothesis*, Blackwell, 1988.

5. Dicks, M.J. and Hatch, N. *The Relationship between Employment and Unemployment*, Bank of England Discussion Paper No. 39, 1989; Disney, R. and colleagues, *Helping the Unemployed: Active labour market policies in Britain and Germany*, Anglo-German Foundation, 1992.

6. For a more extensive review, see: White, M. *Against Unemployment*, Policy Studies Institute, 1991, Chapter 6.

7. Institute for Employment Research (IER), *Review of the Economy and Employment*, IER, 1989.

8. White, M., *op. cit.;* see also Chapter 9.

9. *Employment Gazette*, 1989 Labour Force Survey Preliminary Results, April 1990.

10. *ibid.*

11. McRae, S. *Maternity Rights: the Experience of Women and Employers*, Policy Studies Institute, 1991.

12. Meadows, P., Cooper, H. and Bartholomew, R. *The London Labour Market*, HMSO, 1988.

13. Goldthorpe, J.H. with others, *Social Mobility and Class Structure*, Clarendon Press, 2nd edition, 1988.

14. A follow-up survey to the Oxford Mobility Study in 1983 found that 34 per cent of a national male sample were in higher occupations and 40 per cent in lower occupations, according to the Goldthorpe classification. See: Goldthorpe, J.H. and Payne, C. 'Trends in Intergenerational Class Mobility in England and Wales 1972-83', *Sociology*, vol.20, 1985.

15. See, for example: Daniel, W.W. *The Unemployed Flow*, Policy Studies Institute, 1990.

16. *ibid.;* see also White, M. *Long-term Unemployment and Labour Markets*, Policy Studies Institute, 1983.

17. We could also have included data from 1988 leading up to the current unemployment claim of the sample members, but we wanted the measure of prior unemployment to be somewhat separate from the current claim and so excluded 1988 from the calculation.

18. Data was actually collected for each of the five years 1984 to 1988 inclusive. A measure based on the three central years of this period was chosen as it reduced the possible bias of 1988, in which the individual was partly unemployed by sample definition, and reduced the impact of missing data from the most distant year of recall.

19. Based on those used for the General Household Survey.

20. It should be noted that young people's reports of their educational attainments tend to show a higher level of non-qualification than official statistics based on examination records. This is probably because people tend to discount very low-level qualifications which have little value in working life.

21. White, M. and McRae, S. *Young Adults in Long-term Unemployment*, Policy Studies Institute, 1989; Daniel, W.W., *op.cit.*

22. The detailed results can be found in Table 4.19, *General Household Survey 1989*, HMSO, 1992. Questions on ill-health limiting work have been asked in some Labour Force Surveys, but we know of no published analysis.

23. Daniel, W.W., *op. cit.*

24. This is connected with the notion of 'mismatch' in the labour market. See: Jackman, R., Layard, R. and Savouri, S. *Labour Market Mismatch: A framework for thought*, Centre for Economic Performance (London School of Economics), Discussion Paper No.1, 1990.

Chapter 3

1. Employment Training (ET) was at the time of the study the largest single programme for unemployed people. Priority in ET was given to two groups, (i) those aged 18-24 with six months of unemployment in their current claim, (ii) those aged 18-50 with two years or more of unemployment in their current claim. The timing of Restart interviews at six-monthly intervals from the start of the claim accords with the definition of these two priority groups.

2. The statistical method used was log-linear modelling of multiway tables. Tables were formed from up to seven topics which could be covered in Restart interviews (Job, ET, Restart Course, Jobclub, EAS, Disability advice, Claimant Advisor), and models consisting of the interactions between various three-way and four-way selections of these topics were fitted to this overall table. It was found that many of these higher-order interactions were significant, which indicated that topics tended to be treated in clusters. However, we were unable to reduce the treatment of topics to any usefully simple set of clusters.

3. The statistical technique was logistic regression analysis, sometimes also called logit analysis. The binary dependent variable is transformed to the logistic or log-odds distribution (use of the untransformed binary variable could lead to statistical

estimates which violate the requirement that probabilities lie between 0 and 1). The subsequent analysis can be thought of as a non-linear form of regression analysis. Further details of the estimation procedure can be found in: Aitkin, M. and others, *Statistical Modelling in GLIM*, Clarendon Press (Oxford Statistical Science Series), 1989; see especially 107-118, 167-178.

4. The 'factors' reported here and below should be thought of as multiplying the odds of the outcome in question. An odds-ratio of 1 is the same as the term 'evens' in betting. A factor greater than one means that the outcome becomes 'odds-on' and a factor less than one means that the outcome becomes 'odds-against'. For example, the factor of 1.25 in the present example means that if women were 'evens' to receive a placement after Restart, then men would be 5-to-4 on to receive a placement. Similarly, factors less than one lead to a mutliplicative reduction in the odds or relative odds.

It must be appreciated, however, that since the analysis is non-linear, the net effect of each variable can only be assessed when the values of all other variables in the model are considered at fixed values.

5. The method is as described in notes 3 and 4 above, and the same set of explanatory variables as before was used in the assessments.

6. The proportion in employment at any given point in time will be biased towards those with longer periods of employment by comparison with those having only short periods of employment. Many of those who had had some employment were out of work again by the time of the first survey interview. For further details, see Chapter 5.

7. The technical problem involved in such an analysis is that selection (including self-selection) into a Restart action is likely to be influenced by some of the same factors as influence unemployment outcomes. Some of these factors will be observed and measured, others will be unobserved, and there will tend to be a non-zero correlation between the error term of the estimation equation for selection into a Restart action and the error term of the estimation equation for the unemployment outcome. One should proceed by means of a two-stage least squares analysis which permits this error correlation to be removed. It is well

known, however, that a two-stage procedure is only effective where the model at the first stage is a reasonably good one, i.e. it accounts for a fairly substantial proportion of the variance. This condition is clearly not satisfied in the present case since the study did not focus upon this aspect. In addition, we here have not a simple selection case, but a case of multiple selection or multiple choice (since there are numerous Restart actions). This would lead to a highly complex modelling problem.

8. The analysis followed the same pattern as those described in notes 3-4. Issues of selectivity or endogeneity were ignored.

Chapter 4

1. Because many individuals had not been unemployed claimants during 1982-87, but spent the entire period of the study as unemployed claimants, there was a substantial clump at the value of +100 per cent on the outcome measure. It was therefore necessary to analyse the data by means of a censored regression or Tobit model (see also Chapter 1). The t-statistic for the control group coefficient (the Restart group being taken as the reference group) was 2.66, which on a one-tailed test (see Chapter 1) has $p < 0.005$. (With an OLS model, the Restart effect is estimated at -4.3 per cent, but this is certainly an inefficient estimate as shown by a t-statistic of only 2.29.) The t-statistics for the other significant effects were as follows: change in local unemployment, -5.06; inner city area, 2.24; female, 8.27; aged 25-34, -3.39; aged 45-54, 4.63; aged 55 or over, 8.42; non-respondent, -6.91. It can be argued that survey non-response is endogenous with respect to unemployment, hence it is not sufficient to include it simply as a control variable. Accordingly, an alternative specification in which non-response was taken as an endogenous effect was also used; non-response was modelled as a function of age and change in local unemployment. The t-statistic for the control group was little affected by this re-specification, falling to 2.34 ($p < 0.01$). See also notes 3-4 below.

2. The analysis used was again a censored regression (Tobit) model. The t-statistic for the control group was 2.45, which on a one-tailed test assumption has $p < 0.01$. This analysis excluded from the control group those who stated that they received a Restart

interview. As discussed in Chapter 1, it is defensible to retain these individuals in the control group. With this alternative definition of the control group, the t-statistic for the control group falls somewhat to 1.92, which remains significant on a one-tailed test assumption, p <0.05.

3. Green, W.H. *Econometric Analysis*, Macmillan, 1990; Maddala, G. *Limited - Dependent and Qualitative Variables in Econometrics*, Cambridge University Press, 1983.

4. Blundell, R. *Lectures in Microeconometrics*, University College London, mimeo, January 1990.

5. The t-statistic for the selection coefficient, 'lambda', was 0.68 and non-significant. Similarly, the estimated correlation between the error terms in the selection model was only 0.03. Our interpretation is that the sample selection model cannot be sustained; however, as many analysts persist with selection models when lambda and rho are non-significant, we continue with the results for the benefit of those who would attach weight to them.

6. The t-statistic for the control group was 1.93, one-tailed p <0.05.

7. The t-statistic for the control group was estimated as 5.9, with p <0.001. The other t-statistics for the explanatory variables were as follows: rate of turnover in local labour market, -9.5; change in local unemployment, -7.5; inner city area, 7.1; start-week of claim, 4.8; female, -6.3; aged 25-34, 3.2; aged 35-44, 9.2; aged 45-54, 9.3; aged 55 or over, 4.2; percentage of time unemployed 1982-87, 22.0. Non-response was not included as a variable in this model. The underlying distribution was assumed to be exponential. Repeating the analysis with a Weibull distribution assumption, we obtained a t-statistic for the control group of 5.39, closely similar to the previous result. Also, the time dependence parameter (lambda) was 0.93, close to the exponential assumption of lambda=1.

8. The t-statistic for the control group was 3.75, p <0.001. The specification for this analysis incorporates the assumption of an underlying exponential distribution. Re-estimating the model with a Weibull distribution assumption, the t-statistic for the control group was 3.58, close to its previous value, and the time

dependence parameter was 0.97, very close to the exponential distribution assumption.

9. The form of analysis used here was the probit model; this assumes that the observed dichotomy arises from a cutting-point on an underlying continuous variable having a normal distribution.

10. This is equivalent to assuming that each other variable in the model interacts with gender (i.e. has different values for men and women) in its effects on 'early exits'.

11. The t-statistic for the control group was 1.73, p <0.05 on the one-tailed criterion.

12. The method of analysis was logistic regression modelling; see Chapter 1.

Chapter 5

1. It is not possible to test the differences simply by considering standard errors or confidence intervals, since all these measures have grossly non-normal distributions.

2. Difference measures are widely used by labour market analysts, especially in analysing wage data. Advantages often obtained are (a) reduction or elimination of the influences of unmeasured variables, in so far as these are constant across the comparison periods, (b) better distributed (more symmetrical) measures. Both these advantages are relevant here.

3. The method of analysis was censored regression (Tobit) modelling. This was necessary because of clustering at the lower limit value of -100 (people who had been continuously employed during 1985-87 but had no employment during the study period). For further details, see notes and references, Chapter 4.

4. The t-statistic for the control group was -0.88. This increased to -1.37 if the 'inclusive' definition of the control group was used (see Chapter 1), but this remained well short of significance.

5. See White, M. and McRae, S. *Young Adults in Long-term Unemployment*, Policy Studies Institute, 1989.

6. The dependent variable and explanatory variables were identical. However, it was found that with the longer time-period, the distribution of the dependent variable was well-centered with few

values at the limit of -100. Accordingly, an OLS model was applied.

7. The OLS analysis, with the 'exclusive' definition of the control group which we have generally preferred, produced an estimate of the difference between the control group and the Restart group of -5.9 percentage points in their time spent in employment (relative to previous employment). The t-statistic was -1.70, which is just significant on a one-tailed test (p <0.05). However, when the 'inclusive' definition of the control group was used, the estimate was reduced to -3.22 percentage points, with a t-statistic of -1.06, clearly non-significant.

8. See Chapter 1 for further details of the approach adopted.

9. With an exponential distribution assumed for survival times, the t-statistic for the control group was 1.7, which on a one-tailed test is just significant (p <0.05).

10. With an exponential distribution assumption, the t-statistic for the control group effect was 2.88, p <0.002 (the control group members took longer to enter employment). This was with the 'exclusive' definition of the control group. Changing to the 'inclusive' definition of the control group hardly affected the result, the t-statistic for the control group becoming 2.78. With a Weibull distribution assumption (and 'exclusive' control group), the t-statistic for the control group was reduced to 2.34, p <0.01 – still highly significant. The time dependency parameter in the latter analysis was 0.62, clearly different from the exponential assumption; this supports the preferability of the Weibull assumption. The coefficient indicates that longer times led to a decreasing chance of entering employment for this sample. This is in accordance with the supposition that exposure to lengthy unemployment itself constitutes a disadvantage, but more sophisticated modelling would be required to strengthen this interpretation.

11. This figure is obtained from estimates made by survey respondents of the number of months spent in each year, 1984-88, on government programmes. The denominator for the percentage excluded time prior to the sixteenth birthday of the respondent and was also adjusted for those reporting they had A-level, equivalent or higher qualifications.

12. The percentage measure had an awkward distribution, since most of the sample had not been on ET (and therefore had a percentage of zero), while the minority who had entered ET by the first interview tended to have spent a large proportion of time in that status. Attempts to fit a Tobit model were unsuccessful due to non-convergence of the estimation algorithm. Accordingly participation in ET was treated as a binary variable and the model fitted was of the logistic regression form.

13. Using our preferred 'exclusive' definition of the control group, we obtained a t-statistic for the control group of -1.58, which falls just short of significance on a one-tailed criterion (p <0.06). Repeating the analysis with the 'inclusive' definition of the control group produced a clearly significant Restart effect, with a t-statistic of -2.26.

14. The form of analysis used was a censored regression (Tobit) model. The t-statistic for the control group estimated effect was -2.07, p <0.02 on a one-tailed criterion. This was with the 'exclusive' definition of the control group; with the 'inclusive' definition, the t-statistic was similar, -2.41.

15. With an exponential distribution assumed for the survival times, the t-statistic for the control group was 2.07, p <0.02 for a one-tailed test. This was with the 'exclusive' control group definition; if an 'inclusive' control group definition was used, the t-statistic was virtually the same (2.02). Introducing a Weibull distribution assumption, however, made more difference than elsewhere in this study. With the 'exclusive' definition, the t-statistic for the control group fell to 1.60, just short of significance (p <0.06), while with the 'inclusive' control group definition the t-statistic was 1.88, significant on a one-tailed criterion (p <0.05). The Weibull formulation depressed the significance level of most explanatory variables in this analysis, and the coefficient of duration dependence was very highly negative at 0.56. This should mean that the longer a person remains out of ET, the lower the chances of entry to it. This is entirely plausible, as there is a clear entry point to ET following six months of unemployment, especially for those aged 18-24.

16. The most widely used approach for a wages analysis would consider the change of earnings from the former employment (or

from a previous employment representative of the individual's previous work history) and the current, post-programme employment. A two-stage model would then be estimated, with sample selection to adjust for differences in those getting jobs and those not getting jobs.

17. For such evidence, see White, M. and McRae, S. *op.cit.*

Chapter 6

1. Because a large proportion of the sample had spent no time in the non-claimant status, it was appropriate to use a censored regression (Tobit) model for this analysis. The t-statistic for the control group was -2.04, p <0.03 on a one-tailed criterion. This was with the 'exclusive' definition of the control group; with the 'inclusive' definition, the t-statistic was very similar, at -2.26.

2. A censored regression model was again applied. The t-statistic with the 'exclusive' definition of the control group was 0.607, far from significance, and with the 'inclusive' definition was virtually the same, 0.602.

3. Using an exponential distribution assumption for the parametric survival model, and the 'exclusive' definition of the control group, the t-statistic was -1.49. Since we had no a priori reason to suppose that Restart would increase entry-times to non-claimant status, a two-tailed test criterion must be applied, and the effect is then clearly non-significant. However, if the 'inclusive' definition of the control group is used, the t-statistic for the control group becomes -2.02, just significant (p <0.05 on a two- tailed test). With a Weibull distribution assumption, the t-statistics are reduced in both cases (to -1.38 and -1.84 respectively), and both are judged non-significant on a two-tailed test. The Weibull parameter signifying time dependence took the value of 0.76, indicating declining probability of entering a non-claimant status with increasing time, and this seems consistent with the other findings of this section.

4. The reason for confining attention to those interviewed at the second stage of the survey was that a full year's information on entry-times to non-claimant status is obtained, with a wider distribution of these times.

Chapter 7

1. This was an OLS regression analysis.

2. No job applications was used as the reference variable; each other level of job applications was treated as a dummy (0,1) variable.

3. The t-statistics for the different levels of job applications were as follows: 1-4 applications, 2.56; 5-10 applications, 2.63; 11-19 applications, 2.46; 20 or more applications, 1.06.

4. The t-statistic for the control group was -2.07, with $p < 0.02$ for a one-tailed test. In part this could derive because job-search acts as a suppressor variable, that is, the Restart effect on employment can only show itself when individuals have a reasonable level of job-search. Another factor in the increased significance of the Restart effect is that the design of this analysis, focusing upon employment in the second half of the study period, may thereby be concentrating on the stage when Restart (and the programmes to which it is linked) are having their full impact.

5. The specification for this analysis incorporated an exponential distribution assumption. The t-statistics for the different levels of job applications were: 1-4 applications, -3.54; 5-9 applications, -7.44; 10-19 applications, -7.94; 20 or more applications, -6.78.

6. The t-statistic for the control group was 1.73, with $p < 0.05$ on a one-tailed test criterion.

7. The method of analysis was ordered probit analysis; this imputes an underlying scaling to the ordered categories on the basis of the frequencies observed. For further details, see Green, W.H. *Econometric Analysis*, Macmillan, 1990.

8. See White, M. and McRae, S. *Young Adults and Long-term Unemployment*, Policy Studies Institute, 1989.

9. Expected value = value of outcome x probability of the outcome occurring.

10. The t-statistic for the control group was -1.48, $p < 0.07$ on a one-tailed test.

11. The t-statistic for the 'submitted not placed' group was 4.87, $p < 0.001$. The analysis used was again an ordered probit model.

12. The use of a two-stage procedure with an ordered probit model is described in Green. W.H. *LIMDEP Version 5.1*, 1989. In principle this is similar to the more customary sample selection model in which the second stage is OLS regression. The correlation between the error terms was estimated at 0.16, which supports the relevance of a selection modelling approach here.

13. See, for example, Narendranathan, W. and Nickell, S. 'Modelling the Process of Job Search', in Nickell, S., Narendranathan, W., Stern, J. and Garcia, J. *The Nature of Unemployment in Britain*, Clarendon Press, 1989.

14. For an introduction to relevant theory, see: Joll, C., McKenna, C., McNab, R. and Shorey, J. *Developments in Labour Market Analysis*, George Allen and Unwin, 1983.

15. See, for example, White M. and McRae, S. *op.cit.*

Chapter 8

1. Relative to a baseline period of previous employment.

2. Layard, R., Nickell, S. and Jackman, R. *Unemployment: Macroeconomic performance and the labour market*, Oxford University Press, 1991, page 477.

3. The two studies are: Dicks, M.J. and Hatch, N. *The Relationship between Employment and Unemployment*, Bank of England Discussion Paper No.39, 1989; Disney, R. and others, *Helping the Unemployed: Active Labour Market Policies in Britain and Germany*, Anglo-German Foundation, 1991, see Chapter 7. Dicks and Hatch used the Bank of England's multi-equation macroeconomic forecasting model as a basis for their investigation. Disney and colleagues used the econometric technique of seemingly unrelated regression analysis to make simultaneous estimates for different unemployment duration groups of the Restart effect upon outflow rates from unemployment.

4. Unless one makes the assumption that the effects of Restart are negative for people with long durations of unemployment. Disney and colleagues, cited above, estimated that the positive effects of Restart increased with duration of unemployment.

5. Crowley-Bainton, T. and White, M. *Employing Unemployed People: How Employers Gain*, Employment Service, 1990.

6. Organisation for Economic Co-operation and Development, *Evaluating Labour Market and Social Programmes: The State of a Complex Art*, OECD, 1991.

7. The OECD cites a total cost of £73 million for the year 1989-90 for the Restart programme, and it is believed that about 3 million interviews are conducted under Restart each year. However, the OECD figure included the costs of Jobclubs, Restart courses and Jobstart allowances in its figure. Separate figures for the costs of these elements are not available. It is apparent that £25 would be an absolute upper limit of the cost per Restart interview, and even £20 may be high. See: Organisation for Economic Co-operation and Development, *Labour Market Policies for the 1990s*, OECD, 1990, Annex B: Country Tables of Labour Market Programmes.

Appendix 1

Restart Programme – Background

1. The Restart programme was launched by the then Manpower Services Commission in nine pilot areas in January 1986. It offered advisory interviews to people unemployed for 12 months or more and claiming benefit and/or National Insurance credits. The programme was introduced nationally in July 1986 and extended to include people unemployed for six months or more in April 1987. Since April 1988, the Government has guaranteed an offer of an advisory interview at six-monthly intervals to everyone unemployed for six months or more.

2. The aim of the Restart programme was, and is, to help longer term unemployed people back into work by:

   • *encouraging* them to be more active in looking for work.

   • *identifying* those who do not satisfy entitlement conditions for receiving benefit.

   • *informing* them about the jobs and other opportunities available.

   During the Restart interview advisers therefore discuss the range of opportunities available to a particular client and agree a course of action to help them get back into employment. In addition a check is made to ensure that the client is meeting the requirements placed on them by the benefit regulations. For those clients who need further support the adviser will arrange a follow up interview. Others may be taken onto a 'caseload' and given a continuing programme of help. Attendance at interviews is obligatory in that failure to attend can affect the individual's entitlement to benefit. Interviews take place in Employment Service *Jobcentres*.

3. Restart interviews were originally carried out by Restart Counsellors. However, with the integration of the job placement and benefit payment services, the role of these advisors became increasingly blurred with that of the Claimant Advisers introduced by the Unemployment Benefit Service in November 1986 to provide advice for unemployed people. As a result the two roles were formally merged in April 1990 to create a multifunctioning officer, called a *Claimant Adviser*. At the same time a 'new framework' for advising claimants was introduced. This included a number of other new measures including:

- the use of 'Back to Work Plans' by all advisers.

- the introduction of reviews and interviews for people reaching 13 weeks of unemployment.

- more systematic follow up of clients who do not attend or start a job or programme they were referred to.

- a programme of intensive help for those remaining unemployed after two years.

Appendix 2

Details of Terms Used within the Restart Programme

The following information is based on definitions used within the Employment Service, or in publications of the Service.

A. Terms used to designate outcomes following the Restart interview

Placed
The client was submitted to and accepted either a job or a place on a programme (see section B below for further details).

Submitted but not placed
The client was submitted to one of the above but was not placed.

Referred to DRO, ERC, CA, etc
The client was referred to another specialist service which complements the role of the Restart Counsellor.

Claimant Advisors can give specialist advice on in-work benefits, and offer counselling on a regular and frequent basis.

Disabled Resettlement Officers work with disabled jobseekers, giving general advice and matching their caseload with suitable vacancies.

Employment Rehabilitation Centres run short assessment courses (1-5 days) which are used to judge the client's suitability for rehabilitation and identify the type of programme best suited to the client's needs. Clients can then progress to a full rehabilitation course, lasting on average 6-7 weeks.

Note: Subsequent to the study, the role of Restart counsellors was merged with that of Claimant Advisors.

Declined not referred
The client declined all offers made by the counsellor but was not referred on to the Unemployment Benefits Office (UBO) for refusal of suitable employment or because their availability was in question.

Declined, referred
The client declined all offers and was referred on to the UBO.

UBO's are notified of clients who refuse a suitable submission to a job, or approved training.

Offer not appropriate
Staff may judge that a formal offer from the range of options offered through Restart to be inappropriate. Cases generally fall into two categories.

(i) clients who are already on, or about to start on a specific programme which will not take them directly off the register, e.g, membership of a Jobclub, and for whom there are no other suitable opportunities.

(ii) those who are about to leave the register.

Excused interview
Clients may be excused attendance at the Restart interview if they either

(i) state that they have already signed off

   or

(ii) declare an intention to sign off within four weeks of the date of the interview.

Fail to attend
Clients who fail to respond to two invitations to a main Restart interview, and who have not been excused attendance, are referred to the UBO for possible disallowance action.

Availability
A client is defined as available for work if they can start work straight away, or at 24 hours notice if they are caring for a dependant or involved in some form of voluntary work. Other conditions are that the client is not restricting their chances of getting work because of:
- the type of work they are looking for;
- the hours they can work
- rate of pay they are willing to consider
- places they are prepared to go to work.

B. Examples of programmes for which Restart acts as a gateway

Restart Courses
Aimed at clients who have been unemployed for six months or more, courses help them plan a way back to work by exploring all the options in more depth.

Additional places have been made available subsequent to the study. The aim is also to provide specialised courses for people with particular needs eg. literacy problems, ex-prisoners, and managerial and executive people.

Employment Training
ET is aimed primarily at long term unemployed claimants in need of vocational training before starting work again. Those aged 18-24 years with six months of continuous unemployment are guaranteed a place. Priority is also given to those aged 18-50 with two years of continuous unemployment. There is a variety of provision for other special circumstances, e.g., women returning to the labour market.

ET can continue for up to one year, and the average period is six months.

Jobclubs
Jobclubs aim to help long term unemployed jobseekers who have adequate qualification and experience, and who retain sufficient motivation to persevere with intensive job search activity.

Since the study, an extra 40,000 places per year have been made available bringing the total to 187,000. Executive jobseekers are able to benefit from separate specialist or mainstream jobclubs.

Enterprise Allowance
This programme provides financial support for one year, for unemployed people beginning their own business. There are also introductory short courses and advisory services to help such people.

Job interview guarantee
A programme designed to help long term unemployed people (six months or more), who are motivated and ready to re-enter employment immediately. JIG aims to form links with local employers to give claimants a guaranteed interview. In some variations of this programme, benefit support continues for unemployed people attending short courses to familiarise themselves with the work on offer from particular employers.

Disability services
Unemployed people with problems of disability, limiting the type of work they can do, can be referred to specialist services and provision through a Disablement Resettlement Officer. Advice is also provided on entitlement to special financial benefits. Support includes the Job Introduction programme, which provides a subsidy to employers offering a trial period of work, and Special Aids to Employment, under which equipment is loaned to disabled individuals to help them with their work. In addition, eligibility conditions for the main programmes are often relaxed for people with disabilities.

Appendix 3

Statistical Checks on Control Group Bias

1. Relationship of control group to personal and labour market characteristics variables

To test for the presence of bias, the variables found to relate to unemployment outcomes in the present study were used as explanatory factors in a multivariate analysis, in which the dependent variable was membership of the control group (a binary variable). A logistic regression model was used. The analysis was repeated for two alternative definitions of the control group, (a) 'exclusive', which involved removal of those who had taken part or said they had taken part in a Restart interview, (b) 'inclusive', in which the control group was left exactly as originally defined.

The variables used in the models were the complete set described in Chapter One: labour market turnover (FPS), change in local employment rate (DUN8890), inner city area (IC), start week of claim (SWEEK), gender (FEM), age-groups (four dummy variables), educational qualification (AQY), vocational qualification (TQY), driving licence (DVLY), ethnic group (three dummy variables), marital status (two dummy variables), number of dependant children (DKID), children aged under five (two dummy variables), limiting illness of disability (HTHY), householder in local authority housing (LARY), percentage of time as unemployed claimant 1982-87 (MOPC), percentage of time in employment 1985-97 (JPC3).

The results for the two models were similar. Each showed that the logistic regression equation as a whole was non-significant. The results are summarised below.

(a) 'Exclusive' definition of control group
Log-likelihood: -841
Restricted (slopes=0) log-likelihood: -851
Chi-square for regression: 20.3, on 24 d.f., p=0.68.

Significant (p <0.05) parameters:
constant term, b=-2.42, s.e.=0.63, t=-3.84.

(b) 'Inclusive' definition of control group
Log-likelihood: -1052.3
Restricted (slopes=0) log-likelihood: -1063.8
Chi-square for regression: 22.9, on 24 d.f., p=0.52.

Significant (p <0.05) parameters:
constant term, b=-2.81, s.e.=0.54. t=-5.15.
FPS, b=4.99, s.e.=2.11, t=2.37.

2. Relationship of control group to attitudes

The survey interview contained a self-completion form with 13 attitudinal questions (two of which were answered only by those married or living with a partner). The items had five-point agreement scales, with 'don't know' allocated an additional code. Each item was cross-tabulated by Restart/control group membership, to form a 6 x 2 contingency table, and the Pearson chi-square coefficient was computed, with 5 degrees of freedom in each case. This sequence of 13 analyses was repeated for (a) the 'exclusive' definition of the control group, (b) the 'inclusive' definition. The results are summarised. Significant (p <0.05) coefficients are asterisked; others are non-significant. The N for each table is 4,677 except for the last two, where it is 2,143.

(a) 'Exclusive' definition of control group

Item	Chi-square	p
I would start work straight away if I could get a job	10.5	0.06
I feel alright about being out of work because so many other people are out of work too	7.1	0.21
I get very bored having no work to do	4.1	0.53

Not having a job is making me lose my confidence about ever going back to work	2.1	0.83
There aren't many jobs around for people like me	7.2	0.20
I am worried about having to repay money I owe, when I start earning again	6.0	0.31
It would be difficult for me to earn a wage high enough to be worth my while working	3.0	0.70
For someone like me, benefits give more security than trying to earn a wage	0.5	0.99
A person's wage should be enough to live on without needing benefit at the same time	2.2	0.83
Benefit is money I've worked for in the past	6.5	0.26
It's worth my accepting a low wage if I can prove myself to an employer	13.6	0.02*
If I found a job my partner would find it worth looking for one	2.3	0.81
It's not worth my partner working while I'm unemployed and receiving benefit	4.4	0.49

The full table for the significant item above was as follows:

	Restart group	**Control group**
	column percentages	
It's worth my accepting a low wage if I can prove myself to an employer		
Strongly agree	20	26
Agree	26	17
Neither agree nor disagree	16	20
Disagree	13	11
Strongly disagree	24	25
Don't know	1	1
N	4439	238

The apparent difference between the control group and the Restart group chiefly resides in the strength of agreement.

(b) *'Inclusive' definition of control group*

Item	Chi-square	p
I would start work straight away if I could get a job	6.6	0.25
I feel alright about being out of work because so many other people are out of work too	4.5	0.48
I get very bored having no work to do	4.7	0.45
Not having a job is making me lose my confidence about ever going back to work	3.4	0.64
There aren't many jobs around for people like me	12.8	0.03*
I am worried about having to repay money I owe, when I start earning again	3.2	0.67
It would be difficult for me to earn a wage high enough to be worth my while working	7.2	0.21
For someone like me, benefits give more security than trying to earn a wage	4.1	0.53
A person's wage should be enough to live on without needing benefit at the same time	1.8	0.87
Benefit is money I've worked for in the past	7.0	0.22
It's worth my accepting a low wage if I can prove myself to an employer	7.0	0.22
If I found a job my partner would find it worth looking for one	1.7	0.89
It's not worth my partner working while I'm unemployed and receiving benefit	4.5	0.47

The full table for the significant item above was as follows:

	Restart group	Control group
	column percentages	
There aren't many jobs around for people like me		
Strongly agree	33	36
Agree	21	20
Neither agree nor disagree	14	18
Disagree	16	14
Strongly disagree	16	11
Don't know	1	2
N	4357	320

There is a slight trend in the table, with the control group being more in agreement with the statement.

3. Comparison of Restart effects assessed in the chief models, with 'exclusive' and 'inclusive' definitions of the control group

Significant t-statistics are asterisked. In most cases a one-tailed test criterion is applied.

Outcome	Model	Control group definition	
		'Exclusive'	'Inclusive'
		t-statistics for controls	
(a) Total survey including non-respondents (N=8189)			
Change in % time claiming (whole period)	Tobit	n.a.	2.66*
Initial exit-time from claiming (whole period)	Survival	n.a.	5.90*
(b) Those at first survey interview (N=4807)			
Change in % time claiming (whole period)	Tobit	1.92*	2.45*

The Restart effect

Initial exit-time from claiming (whole period)	Survival	3.75*	4.23*
Change in % time in job (first 6 months)	Tobit	-0.88	-1.37
Participation in ET etc. (first 6 months)	Logit	-1.58	-2.26*
% time in non-claimant status (first 6 months)	Tobit	-2.04*	-2.26*
(c) Those at second survey interview (N=3419)			
Change in % time in job (whole period)	OLS	-1.70*	-1.06
Initial entry-time to job (whole period)	Survival	2.88*	2.78*
% time in ET (whole period)	Tobit	-2.07*	-2.41*
Initial entry-time to ET (whole period)	Survival	2.07*	2.02*
% time in non-claimant status (whole period)	Tobit	0.61	0.60
Initial entry-time to non-claimant status (whole period)	Survival	-1.49	-2.02*